Parliamentary Office of
Science and Technology

SAFETY IN NUMBERS?

- Risk Assessment in Environmental Protection

June
1996

The Parliamentary Office of Science and Technology is an office of Parliament which serves both Houses by providing objective and independent information and analyses on science and technology-related issues of concern to Parliament. POST has been funded by Parliament since 1 April 1993; before then, the office had been supported for four years by donations under the auspices of the Parliamentary and Scientific Committee.

Primary authors: Gary Kass, Dr Michael Norton

Acknowledgements

The Parliamentary Office of Science and Technology would like to thank ....
for providing information and expert comment:-
Advisory Committee on Business and the Environment
Department of the Environment
Deregulation Unit
Centre for Environmental Strategy, University of Surrey
Centre for Hazard and Risk Management, Loughborough University
Centre for Risk and Environmental Management, University of East Anglia
Confederation of British Industry
Council for the Protection of Rural England
Environmental Industries Commission
Environment Agency
Environment Council
Friends of the Earth
Health and Safety Executive
Her Majesty's Inspectorate of Pollution (HMIP)
Greenpeace
National Society for Clean Air and Environmental Protection
Royal Commission on Environmental Pollution
Royal Society
Sir Frederick Warner FRS FEng

Cover photographs:

Top:	Petrochemical complex
Courtesy:	Her Majesty's Inspectorate of Pollution (HMIP)
Bottom:	Problems of risk perception: the case of the Brent Spar
Courtesy:	Greenpeace

CONTENTS

BOXES, TABLES AND FIGURES

1   INTRODUCTION

Few would dispute that life is risky, although many might disagree on how large or important a given risk might be. For instance, are the risks from nuclear power greater or less than those from chemicals in the environment, driving a car, eating beef, working on a building site or smoking 40 cigarettes a day? In our complex society, virtually all decisions involve some implicit or explicit assessment of the risks involved - to identify the consequences of an intended activity; estimate the chances that the consequences might be realised; and weigh up the risks against the potential benefits. The ways in which society manages and controls risk to its population affect everyone.

Formal systems of risk assessment have long been a feature of work-place health and safety regulation (e.g. exposure to radiation) and in engineering design (e.g. design life of structures). In environmental protection, risk assessment has had a more limited application (e.g. setting standards for some toxic chemicals) but is now being used increasingly in other areas alongside established methods such as cost-benefit analysis and environmental assessment. However, no method of predicting environmental impacts or costs and benefits of different levels of pollution control is absolutely certain, and risk assessment has its own problems.

The debate over how far environmental and consumer protection should rely on more formal methods of risk assessment coincides with a drive towards using risk assessment as part of the Deregulation Initiative, through which the costs and benefits of legislation must be appraised. Also, the formation of the Environment Agency in England and Wales (and the Scottish Environmental Protection Agency, SEPA) raises questions over how readily the disparate cultures and methods used by the Agency's predecessors will be integrated within the one Agency.

Although risk assessment may appear at first glance to be a somewhat arcane subject, there are several reasons why this may have a bearing on matters of interest to Parliament. Firstly, as recent bouts of public alarm over beef, babies milk, etc., reveal only too well, everyone is affected by risk and may go to great lengths to avoid certain risks. These public perceptions feed back into the priorities assigned by regulators and may have substantial public expenditure implications.

Secondly, what risk assessment is trying to achieve is a common framework whereby society can get the best value for money from its investment in protecting health or the environment. It is questionable whether it makes sense to spend £10M reducing a very low risk to an even lower one, when much more damaging activities remain unchanged.

Thirdly, in considering how best the Environment Agency can fulfil its functions, the Government will lay (in mid-June) before Parliament draft guidance on the Agency's objectives and how it can contribute to sustainable development. This guidance follows a draft published by the Department of the Environment in December 1995 (1), in which the Government required *inter alia* that the Agency should use the best scientific information available, applying the 'precautionary principle' where appropriate. This will require the

Agency to develop sound techniques of analysis - including assessing risks and taking account of the costs and benefits of its decisions.

In view of these considerations, and the wider debate about the increasing role of risk assessment in policy formulation and decision-making, the Board of the Parliamentary Office of Science and Technology (POST) decided that POST should examine how risk assessment is used in environmental protection and how this may influence the emerging Agency[1].

The report begins by looking at the background to the Agency, and reviews current practices in the use of risk assessment and other appraisal methods. The report then examines how the Agency might use risk assessment in the future. Finally, issues are discussed that consider the strengths and weaknesses of risk assessment, and how the system can deal with the inherent limitations of science in decision-making. In recent years, public confidence in the risk assessment process and regulating agencies has become an increasingly important aspect, and ways are also discussed in which this can be encouraged and the risk assessment process adapted to incorporate better communication and public participation.

---

[1] While the focus of this report is on the Environment Agency, many of the issues raised are also likely to affect the Scottish Environmental Protection Agency.

2.1   Introduction

Over the past ten years, many agencies and organisations (perhaps most notably the Royal Commission on Environmental Pollution, RCEP (2) and the House of Commons Select Committee on the Environment (3)) have highlighted a lack of a strategic and consistent approach to environmental pollution; with a number of existing agencies responsible for different aspects of the environment. Consequently, there have been calls for a single, integrated agency that can tackle protection of the environment coherently and systematically, and to this end the 1995 Environment Act established separate agencies for England and Wales (the Environment Agency) and for Scotland (Scottish Environmental Protection Agency, SEPA).

On 1 April 1996 , the Environment Agency took over the responsibilities of its predecessors, whose roles are described in Section 2.2. The Agency will operate with an initial staff of 9,500 people and will operate in its first year with a budget of £550M. The sources of the Agency's funding and areas of expenditure for 1996/7 are shown in **Figures 2.1a and 2.1b.** These show that the majority (46%) of the budget will be allocated to flood defences (a continuation of the National River Authority's major spend in this area). A further 30% will be spent on pollution prevention and control, 15% on water resources and 6% on fisheries, navigation, conservation and recreation. 3% of the first year's budget will be to cover start-up costs. This expenditure is matched by funding, the majority (68%) of which will come from direct charges (as flood defence levies on local authorities; charges for water abstraction and pollution control; income from recreation; and licence fees for angling and navigation). The remainder of the funding will come from grant-in-aid from government departments (Department of the Environment, Ministry of Agriculture, Fisheries and Food and the Welsh Office).

FIGURE 2.1   ENVIRONMENT AGENCY FUNDING AND EXPENDITURE, 1996/7

(a) FUNDING

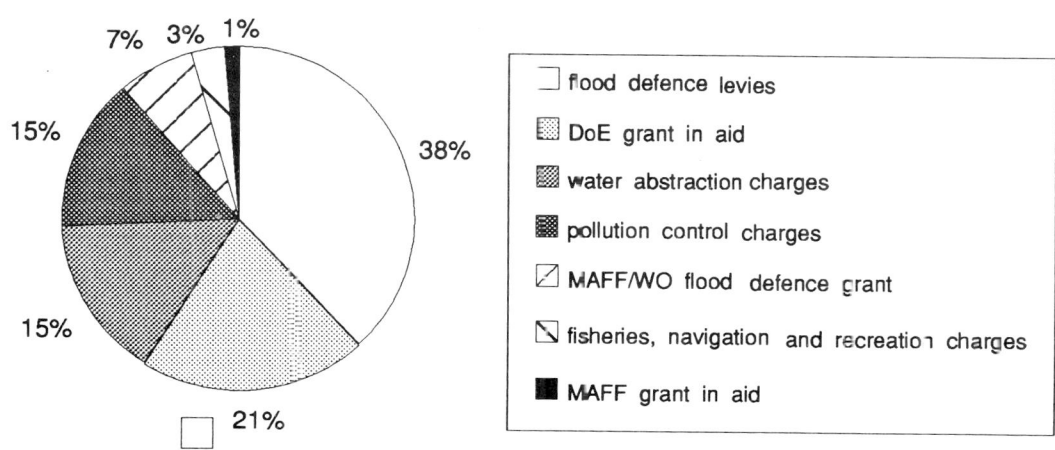

(b) EXPENDITURE

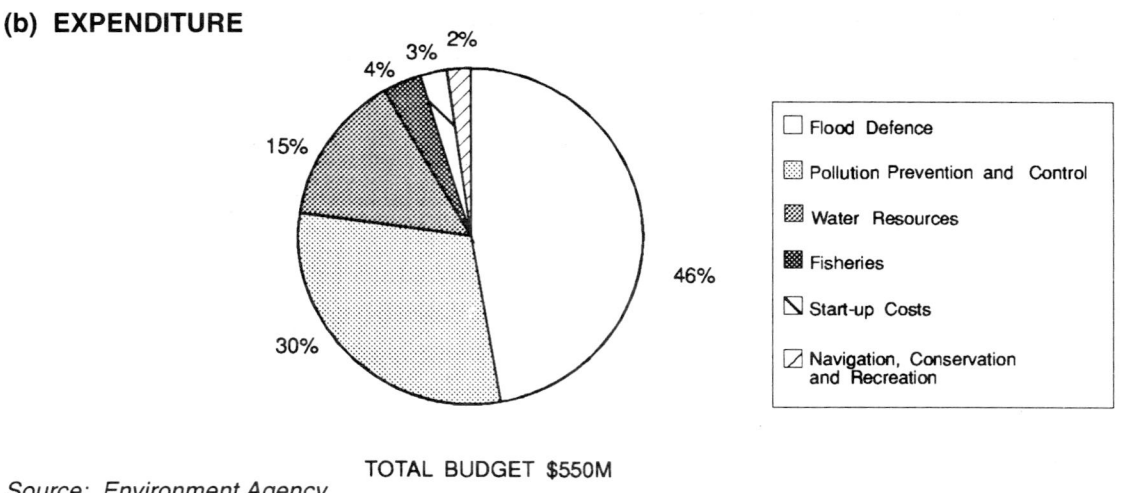

- ☐ Flood Defence
- ▢ Pollution Prevention and Control
- ▨ Water Resources
- ▧ Fisheries
- ◹ Start-up Costs
- ◺ Navigation, Conservation and Recreation

TOTAL BUDGET $550M

Source: Environment Agency

2.2   The Agency's Predecessors

The Environment Agency has been formed by bringing together Her Majesty's Inspectorate of Pollution (HMIP), the National Rivers Authority (NRA), the local authority Waste Regulation Authorities (WRAs) and the parts of the Department of the Environment (DoE) dealing with contaminated land and the technical aspects of waste management. This section describes the evolution of these bodies and how they approached their duties to protect the environment. A more detailed review of the risk assessment methods used by the Agency's predecessors is given in Section 3.4.

HMIP has the longest history of the Agency's predecessors - going back to the 19th Century when the Alkali Inspectorate was established to control pollution from one particularly dirty industrial sector. Consequently, HMIP's methods have evolved over a long time, and have incorporated a number of numerical, engineering and science-based techniques, under a general policy of requiring steady improvements by industry in controlling (mainly air) pollution (according to the principle of Best Practicable Means, BPM). In 1990, the Environmental Protection Act broadened the regime for industrial pollution control by introducing Integrated Pollution Control (IPC). This required that the more polluting industries had to take account of releases of pollution to the environment as a whole (i.e. air, water and land), and also how pollution could move between these media. IPC also established the principle that releases should be **prevented** as a first priority; where this was not possible, they should be minimised and made harmless.

The IPC process identifies current best practice for industrial processes and sets limits on the concentrations of pollutants that can be released, based on state-of-the-art techniques and technologies. Although aimed at a more holistic approach, the Environmental Protection Act restricted HMIP to applying IPC to **individual industrial processes** only and it could not take account of more strategic objectives for environmental quality within whole industrial areas. HMIP was also responsible for the control of radioactive substances and the disposal of radioactive wastes (Section 3.4.1), and also acted as a statutory consultee in other forms of environmental regulation and control, such as planning applications, waste management licences and discharge consents.

The **NRA** was established in 1989 under the Water Act as one of the regulators of the privatised water industry in England and Wales (the others were the Office of Water Services (OFWAT) which regulates prices, and the Drinking Water Inspectorate (DWI) which ensures the safety of drinking water). As the replacement to the Regional Water Authorities, the NRA was given a wide range of duties to protect the water environment, including controlling water quality, managing water resources and flood defences, promoting angling, navigation and recreation, and advising on applications for planning consent, waste management licences and IPC authorisations. It managed water pollution by setting both limits on the quantities and concentrations of pollutants in effluent discharges and also adopting more general objectives to improve water quality. The NRA controlled both small and large discharges of sewage and industrial wastes into streams, rivers, lakes, estuaries and coastal waters.

In terms of regulatory approach, the Regional Water Authorities had placed much reliance on uniform 'end of pipe' standards for whole types of discharges (e.g. the standard 20/30 biochemical oxygen demand and suspended solids limits for sewage works). In more recent years the NRA evolved a more strategic and integrated view of the water environment as a whole, applying site-specific standards and aiming to protect the many uses to which water is put across whole river basins (integrated river basin management, IRBM).

The 87 **WRAs** were formed in 1990 under the Environmental Protection Act as part of the separation of the operational and regulatory aspects of waste disposal carried out by English and Welsh local authorities. The responsibilities of the WRAs ranged from controlling the disposal of household and industrial waste in landfills to licensing waste management facilities such as scrap-yards, waste transfer stations and civic amenity sites. Some WRA areas had large numbers of waste management facilities, while others had relatively few, so the approach taken varied, depending on the resources and expertise available. Some WRAs operated sophisticated methods to appraise and regulate waste management in their areas, while others were restricted to simpler qualitative methods, often relying on centrally produced guidance from DoE but using professional judgement and local knowledge. In the past, waste management also suffered from a confusion over what constituted 'waste', and there was also some blurring of the responsibilities of the WRAs with other regulators. For instance, the NRA often took responsibility for the water pollution aspects of landfill design, and there was often confusion over the boundaries of responsibility between HMIP and the WRAs when deciding who should regulate industrial wastes.

The DoE's responsibility for **contaminated land** goes back to the 1970s when the Government established the Interdepartmental Committee on the Redevelopment of Contaminated Land (ICRCL), and the DoE produced information and advice about guidelines and standards on acceptable levels of contaminants in soil. POST has previously examined some of the issues in controlling contaminated land (4), and in summary, the regime is based on guidelines from the ICRCL which set 'trigger levels' for 20 contaminants for a range of land uses. Concentrations below a lower band (the 'threshold trigger level') meant that soil could be treated as though it was not contaminated, and levels above a limit (the 'action trigger level') meant that some remediation was required. Between these two levels, the DoE recommended that professional judgement should be used to assess the significance of the risks posed by the contamination, and to decide on the best course of

---

action. The Environment Agency now has the responsibility for producing a national strategy for contaminated land in conjunction with local authorities, and to help this, the Government will produce statutory guidance setting out how contaminated land should be defined and identified; who will be responsible for cleaning up contaminated sites, and how the costs of clean-up should be paid.

2.3   The New Agency's Mission

The principal aim of the Agency given in the Government's draft statutory guidance (provided under Section 4 of the Environment Act 1995) is *"to protect or enhance the environment taken as a whole so as to make a contribution towards attaining the goal of sustainable development."* The Agency is also given statutory objectives which can be summarised as follows:

- Taking an integrated approach to environmental protection and enhancement.
- Working with others in close and responsive relationships and providing clear and readily accessible information.
- Using clear and effective procedures and high professional standards, based on sound science, information and analysis.
- Adopting good environmental and management practices and providing value for money.
- The Government requires that to meet the goals of sustainable development, the Agency should:
  - Take an **holistic approach** - taking account of the interactions and effects of pollutants discharged into the air, water or land
  - Take a **long-term perspective** - particularly on effects which may be irreversible, or which affect future generations.
  - Maintain **biodiversity** - including sites of nature conservation importance protected by law and non-designated sites which are still important.
  - Encourage industry (through partnerships) **to adopt improved technologies and management techniques.**
  - Develop **close and responsive relationships** with the public, local authorities, representatives of local communities and regulated businesses.
  - Provide clear and readily accessible advice and information and become a recognised centre of knowledge and expertise.

In implementing the Agency's primary aims of **protecting and enhancing the environment as a whole** and contributing to **sustainable development**, the Agency aims to bring together the traditions of its predecessors into a new culture that takes a strategic, long-term view, rather than the reactive approach to environmental protection that has been the hallmark of some environmental regulation in the past. The Agency will also emphasise *"high professional standards"*, and undertake to work on the basis of *"sound science"*.

The general aspects of the Agency's task are worthy of special note. Firstly, the guidance recognises that there are inherent uncertainties in our knowledge of the environment and that the agency will need to consider the **precautionary principle (PP)** in deciding whether to act to prevent environmental damage. As discussed in **Box 2.1**, there is still some debate over the circumstances under which the principle will be applied.

BOX 2.1 THE PRECAUTIONARY PRINCIPLE

The Precautionary Principle has been used increasingly following the 1992 Earth Summit in Rio de Janiero, where it was defined as: *"Where there are threats of serious or irreversible damage, lack of full scientific certainty shall not be used as a reason for postponing cost-effective measures to prevent environmental degradation."*

Putting the principle into practice means, therefore, that the terms 'threats', 'damage', 'cost-effectiveness' and 'certainty' are clarified, and so the risks involved need to be assessed. The PP means, therefore that action may be needed without full scientific evidence or a strict definition of the risks involved. For instance, in the cases of global warming, ozone-layer depletion and the possible link between BSE and CJD, the precise risks involved are not known in detailed scientific terms, but they are generally considered serious enough to justify action. There are, however, questions over when the principle should be used.

The Government remains committed to basing action on fact and points out that *"precipitate action on the basis of inadequate evidence is the wrong response"*. However, the draft guidance recognises that *"where potential damage to the environment is both uncertain and significant, it is necessary to act on the basis of the precautionary principle"*. In this context, the Government defined the principle as follows (5):-
"where there are significant risks of damage to the environment, the Government will be prepared to take precautionary action to limit the use of potentially dangerous materials or the spread of potentially dangerous pollutants, even where scientific knowledge is not conclusive, if the likely balance of costs and benefits justifies it".

A similar point was made by the House of Lords Committee on Sustainable Development in its 1995 report (6)-
"Given the factual and scientific uncertainties surrounding many environmental concerns, the difficulties faced by governments as they seek to strike an acceptable balance between the creation of wealth and the protection of the environment should not be underestimated. Clearly, when the risks of irreversible environmental damage are high, and the cost penalties of action are minimal, the precautionary principle justifies a decisive response. In other circumstances, however, where a lesser risk is associated with a potentially very expensive precautionary response, it could well be better to promote further scientific research than to embark upon premature action".

Secondly, the Agency will be expected to contribute to **sustainable development** - the concept was first put forward in 1987 by the World Commission on Environment and Development (the "Brundtland Commission") (7) and defined as *"development that meets the needs of the present without compromising the ability of future generations to meet their own needs."* In summary, sustainable development aims to secure higher standards of living through economic development, while protecting and enhancing the environment and quality of life both now and for future generations.

The concept was developed further in 1992, when the UN Conference on Environment and Development (the Earth Summit) was held to encourage many nations to incorporate the concept of sustainable development into their national policies. The UK Government published the UK's strategy for sustainable development in January 1994 (8) and this set out the current situation and policies in the UK and key areas for future action for government, businesses and individuals. The Environment Agency was seen as an important mechanism through which sustainable development could be pursued, and the 1995 Environment Act requires the Government to provide advice to the Environment Agency on its objectives and ways it can contribute to achieving sustainable development.

As mentioned in Section 1, the Government must lay before Parliament the final draft statutory guidance to the Agency on its objectives, and how it will be expected to contribute to sustainable development. This guidance is expected to be laid before Parliament in mid-June, and if no objections are raised within 40 days (i.e. before the end of July 1996), the guidance will be deemed to have been accepted.

Thirdly, another key objective of the Agency is to work with others in "*close and responsive relationships*", increasing its **openness and accountability** further than has been possible in the past. Also, the Agency wishes to provide a more streamlined regulatory system that will not burden businesses with overly complex and bureaucratic procedures. Thus the Agency aims to establish a 'one-stop-shop' culture where third parties need to liaise only with a single contact, rather than having to deal with several regulators each responsible for different functions.

3   HOW DO WE MANAGE RISKS?

3.1   Risk and Safety in Society

Many of today's laws and institutions have come about because people want to feel safe in their day-to-day activities. So, when someone takes a medicine, he or she wants to be assured that it will not kill them or lead to undesirable side-effects, and such concerns led to legislation such as the Medicines Act. Similarly, people expect their working environments to be healthy and safe, and so regulations made under the Health and Safety at Work Act aim to reduce the risks of suffering injury or contracting an illness while at work. Other examples include road safety legislation, controls on other forms of transport (e.g. ferries and aircraft), the safety of food and water, and protecting the environment. Society exerts, therefore, considerable pressures to increase safety or reduce risks from the wide range of activites that make up our modern lives. Moreover, while most people generally accept that it is not possible to guarantee a life absolutely free of risk all the time, the size of that risk and its acceptability can be a fruitful source of controversy.

Legislation to increase safety or reduce risk is very diverse because it has evolved separately in different regulatory areas. In some areas (e.g. air quality), regulatory regimes overlap and there can be scope for regulations to impose different safety standards for the same substance in different circumstances. For instance, under health and safety legislation the maximum concentration of benzene in air to which someone can be exposed at work is 5,000 parts per billion (ppb), but for environmental protection, the DoE's long-term goal is to reduce ambient benzene concentrations to 1 ppb. While there are good reasons for having different standards for different purposes, these (and many other) standards have been derived using different methods to meet the objectives of the particular regulatory regime (e.g. to take account of the different groups at risk), and this diverse approach leads to questions over whether safety standards can be too high in some areas and too low in others. Recently, therefore, pressure has grown for safety standards to be based on a more consistent approach by making sure that regulatory actions are proportionate to the risks involved[2].

This section thus describes the general principles of how risks are assessed, reviews how they are assessed by Government departments, and highlights some of the key themes in assessing risks to the environment.

3.2   General Principles of Risk Assessment

Professional and public use of the term 'risk' often differs. For the engineer, it may be a precise figure (for example, the failure rate of a component in a bridge may be one in a 100 million). For a member of the public it may be a much more qualitative term - climbing is 'risky', and crossing the road can be risky, but it would be much less common for someone to express that general concept in terms of probabilities. Nevertheless, from a practical point

---

[2] In this context, the RCEP is currently examining the basis on which environmental (including consideration of health and safety) standards are set, and is expected to publish its findings before the end of 1996.

of view (9) assessing risks can be seen as pinning down the probability of an event as far as possible to help make decisions in the face of uncertainty. The Royal Society Study Group on Risk (10) recognised this, but adopted a definition of risk most suited for those scientists and engineers who derive numerical values for risks - namely that *"risk is the probability that a particular adverse event occurs during a stated period of time, or results from a particular challenge"*. The British Standard BS 4778 1991 adopts a similar definition, but notes that 'risk' can have a number of meanings, depending on the specific area where it is applied.

Assessing risks is not straightforward, and can perhaps best be understood as a circular process with three main stages (identification, evaluation and management of risks), with communication in the centre, informing and influencing each stage, as illustrated in **Figure 3.1**. This section describes each of the elements, and draws together the key features of the whole process.

FIGURE 3.1 THE RISK ASSESSMENT PROCESS

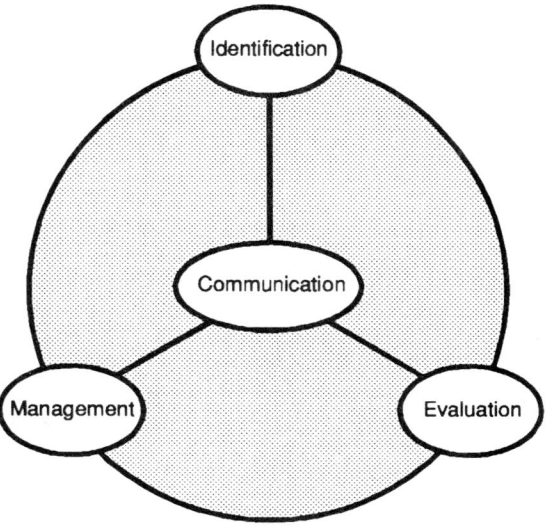

Source: based on (11)

3.2.1   Risk Identification

To illustrate the concept of risk it is useful to start with an example - a proposal to build a new chemical factory in a town. The first point to note is that because the factory would use and make chemicals known to be toxic (rather than making soft toys for example), there is an implicit danger (or hazard) associated with the proposal. The second point is that there is a chance (however small) that the components and equipment in the factory might malfunction (e.g. a valve could become clogged and fail to close), and this might cause the release of toxic gas, harming or killing people. This risk from the factory can be defined, therefore, as the combination of the hazard (the possibility of a release of toxic gas during the manufacture of chemicals) with the chance (or probability) of it happening in a given period. **Box 3.1** describes in more detail what is meant by probability.

Of course, returning to our chemical factory example, there may be other risks than a release of toxic gas, and a more formal process for identifying risks has been developed which breaks the procedure down into a number of elements, as described in **Table 3.1**.

BOX 3.1   THROWING DICE - AN EXAMPLE OF PROBABILITY

People often do not know the outcome of a particular event, and this uncertainty leads to actions which have a certain chance of success or failure, such as betting on the throw of a dice. The chance of a particular outcome can be calculated as a mathematical **probability**. For instance, the chance of throwing a 6 on a single six-sided dice is 1 in 6, and the chance of throwing two successive sixes is 1 in 36 (i.e.1/6 multiplied by 1/6).

However, these probabilities - like betting odds - do not **predict** outcomes, but merely state the chances that they will occur. Thus, a 6 will not always show once if you throw a dice 6 times - there is a greater chance of a 6 not turning up at all (odds of 3 to 1), but a much lower chance that it turns up 6 times out of 6 (odds of 46,656 to 1). Therefore, the best that can be made of probabilities are that they allow comparisons to indicate the relative likelihood of events, but do not predict them. But what do probabilities mean in the 'real' world? Here, we can look at two examples: winning the National Lottery jackpot and dying in a road traffic accident.

As with the dice example the chance of picking the 6 winning numbers in the National Lottery has been calculated from a mathematical formula that describes all the possible ways in which the winning numbers picked. In the Lottery, there are roughly 14 million ways in which 6 numbers can be picked out of 49, so the chance of picking the 6 winning numbers is 1 in 14 million.

On the other hand, there are situations where mathematical formulae are not available for calculating probabilities because of the complexities of the systems involved. In these cases, people resort to empirical evidence of what has happened before, and predict the future on this basis. For example, historically there are roughly 4000 road deaths each year out of a population of 56 million, so the risk of dying is about 1 in 14,000 each year, averaged over the entire UK population. The fact that someone is 1000 times more likely to be killed in a road accident than to win the National Lottery raises an interesting question about how people actually take account of probabilities in their lives.

Most people accept that there is a degree of risk involved when using the roads, but consider the benefits of travelling to outweigh the risks. Similarly, when buying a National Lottery ticket, the benefits of winning a jackpot of £10M are clearly seen to outweigh the risks involved in putting up a £1 stake, despite the extremely low probability of winning. Here, a crucial factor is exemplified by the National Lottery marketing slogan "It Could Be You" - where emphasis is on the word 'could'. While this statement is true, it refers to a probability that in other walks of life, would be considered as 'virtually impossible'. Indeed, the risk of being killed by lightning in the UK is 1 in 11 million, but few expect that it will happen to them - despite the fact that it 'could' and is more likely than winning the National Lottery!

TABLE 3.1   RISK IDENTIFICATION

Element of Risk Identification	Example
Describing the intended activity.	Specifying the size and location of the chemical factory; the processes and chemicals used; the existing quality of air; the prevailing weather conditions; and the location of housing, schools, hospitals, etc.
Identifying the implicit dangers.	The chemicals used and made in the factory might be toxic to people or the environment and, therefore, could be considered 'hazardous'.
Identifying the consequences.	The failure of a valve to close or rupture of a pipe might cause the release of potentially toxic gas from the factory that could harm the health of local people.
Estimating the range of the effects.	The rate and concentration at which the gas is released, and the prevailing weather conditions will determine the area and number of people likely to be affected by the gas.
Estimating the likelihood of harm.	Combining the probabilities of the valve failing to close or the pipe to rupture, the gas being released, the wind blowing the gas towards people and the concentration of the gas being high enough to cause harm will provide an overall estimate of risk - both the probability of occurrence and magnitude of the impact in a given period.

Source: (12)

3.2.2   Risk Evaluation

The second stage in the risk assessment process is to determine how socially and politically acceptable the risks identified in the first stage might be. Here, it is important to recognise that different individuals and groups have different perceptions of risks, and research has identified a number of factors which influence how people perceive risks, and how safe certain activities may be. In **Figure 3.2**, one model of how people perceive risks shows that activities found in the upper right-hand corner are perceived to have the greatest risk, and those in the lower left-hand sector to have the least risk, irrespective of the mathematically calculated probabilities of harm. For instance, while the risks of nuclear power are perceived to be greater than those from non-nuclear power, based on available statistics, the opposite is true. Although helpful in rationalising some major differences in perception, this model has been criticised, as many questions remain - e.g. over how risks are defined, perceptions reported, and how individual perceptions can be aggregated to form generalised statements about society's perceptions. Subsequent research has looked at the cultural and social contexts in which people consider risks, and attempts are being made to combine these two approaches.

FIGURE 3.2 SOME FACTORS AFFECTING THE PERCEPTION OF RISKS

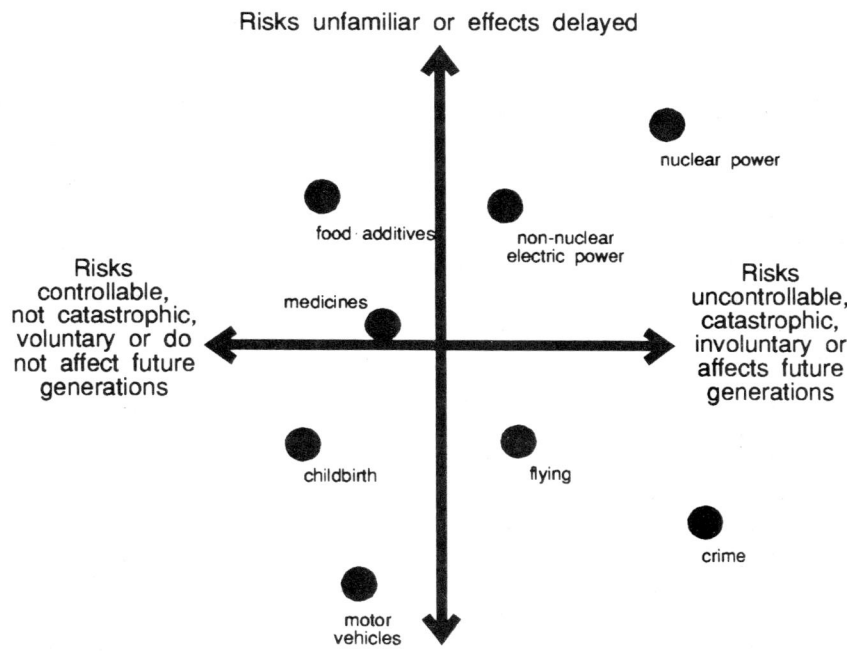

Source: based on (13)

Some of the primary influences on the perception of risks (with reference to the chemical factory example) are:

- **Control** - People are more willing to accept risks they impose upon themselves, or they consider to be 'natural', than to have risks imposed upon them by others. For example, people are willing to go skiing or drive a car, but are much less willing to be exposed to risks from a chemical factory built near them, even though statistically the risk of death or injury from skiing or driving might be much higher than from the factory.

- **Dread and Scale of Impact** - Fear is greatest where the consequences of a risk are likely to be catastrophic rather than spread over time. For example, there would be more concern over a few deaths and injuries from an accident at the chemical factory than over the greater number of deaths that occur every day in road accidents. Thus, risks with a smaller chance of happening, but greater perceived consequences (e.g. the release of toxic gas from the factory) are feared more than those with a greater chance of happening but where the consequences are considered less serious (e.g. injury in a car accident).

- **Familiarity** - People tend to be more willing to accept risks that are familiar to them rather than new risks. For instance, concern over deaths and injuries from car accidents is less than from an accident at the chemical factory, because people tend to feel more familiar with the risks of travelling on the roads than with those stemming from the complex chemical reactions in the factory. Risks from 'natural' radon gas in the home may be seen as more acceptable than exposure to radioactivity from an external industrial source, which may be considered 'unnatural'.

- **Timing** - Risks seem to be more acceptable if the consequences are immediate or likely in the short-term, rather than if they are delayed - especially if the timing of the consequences is unknown, or if they might affect future generations. For instance, injuries from a car accident are immediate and are accepted more readily than exposure to chemicals that could cause cancer or birth defects at some time in the future.

- **Social Amplification and Attenuation** - Concern can be increased because of media coverage or graphic depiction of events. For example, graphic reports of the deaths and injuries from chemical factory accidents (e.g. Bhopal, Seveso and Flixborough) can heighten fear, thus amplifying the perceived risks from any proposal to build a new factory. Alternatively, risks can be played down by social pressures. For example, fears of a new chemical factory would be less in an industrial or economically-deprived area where the social pressure to maintain or create jobs might be greater than in a more prosperous, less industrial area. A good example of this is the case of Elm Energy trying unsuccessfully to site a waste tyre incinerator in Guildford, having successfully sited one in Wolverhampton (14).

- **Trust** - Many researchers now consider that a key factor in the perception of risks is how far the public trusts regulators, policy makers, or industry. If these bodies are open and accountable - being honest, admitting mistakes and limitations and taking account of differing views without disregarding them as emotive or irrational - then the public is more likely to place credibility in them. It can also be easier to lose trust than to gain it. POST has previously reviewed the public's attitudes to science (15), and pointed out that on environmental issues, 82% of people trusted scientists working for environmental organisations, compared to 48% for government scientists and 47% for industry. Similarly, research by the Centre for Environmental and Risk Management (CERM) at the University of East Anglia (16) has shown that people mostly trust information coming from family, friends and doctors, moderately trust environmental/consumer groups and religious leaders, and trust government and industry the least (see Figure 4.2 in Section 4.2).

When dealing with these more subjective aspects, a key question is how far these considerations should affect the reliance placed on the numerical probabilities derived from the first stage of the risk assessment. Some (e.g. 17, 18) have suggested that calculated, 'scientific' probabilities are the only objective measures of the 'real' risk, and that perceptions of risk should be disregarded as being entirely subjective and based on incomplete information, emotion or irrational thought. Others, including the DoE (12), acknowledge that in many areas (e.g. environmental and medical science) the precise knowledge needed for true objectivity may not always be available. Even the 'scientific' aspects of deriving probabilities may involve subjective judgements (9) to varying degrees, and on this basis, some see a role for considering people's perceptions and values in risk assessment. For instance, the Government's Advisory Committee on Business and the Environment (ACBE) has set up a working group to look at how to improve the way Government and industry deal with values and perceptions held by other interested parties (20).

The picture of risks being either wholly 'real' or wholly 'perceived' is probably too simplistic, and the balance will vary with the individual risk involved. Thus engineering calculations are sufficiently robust to be able to predict with confidence that a road bridge is 'safe' and any driver with the perception that it was about to collapse would be acting rather irrationally. On the other hand, in some areas (e.g. the recent concern over the possible transmission of BSE to humans - see POST report 78 (21)), the data on which to base a numerical estimation of risk are not available, and perception becomes the most important factor determining public acceptability of the risk.

There will be many cases, therefore, when, in determining the social and political acceptability of risks, subjective judgements, values and perceptions will need to be taken into account alongside the more traditional scientific information. But the question remains how this should be achieved, and here, an important aspect is how well scientists, decision-makers, interested groups and the wider public can communicate with each other (see Section 3.2.4).

3.2.3   Risk Management

Having identified and evaluated the risks, decisions have to be reached over how acceptable the risks might be, and whether the action needs to be taken - either to eliminate the risks altogether or reduce them to a tolerable level. This is the province of risk management. It is important here to recognise the difference between what might be 'acceptable' (i.e. risks are considered negligible, and people are willing to take them) and what might be 'tolerable' (i.e. people see that risks are significant, but they can be tolerated while efforts are made to reduce them further). Of course, altering the original activity may mean that the assessment cycle should be repeated - identifying and evaluating the risks from the revised activity until agreement is reached on acceptable risk management decisions.

As explained in Section 3.2.1, 'risk' depends on both the potential to cause harm (the hazard) and the likelihood of harm occurring in a given period (the probability), so risks could be reduced by controlling one or both of these. For instance, in our chemical factory example, it may be possible to manage the hazards involved in operating the factory by using less hazardous substances. A real-life example is where chlorofluorocarbons (CFCs), previously used in refrigerators and aerosol sprays, were banned because they damaged the ozone layer, and were replaced initially with hydrochlorofluorocarbons (HCFCs) and subsequently by hydrofluorocarbons (HFCs) which reduced the hazard further[3].

It may also be possible to control the chances of harm occurring, and there are two main ways this could be done:

- **Reduce the likelihood of a hazard occurring.** For example, fit additional safety features at the chemical factory such as back-up valves and devices that fail to a safe state to minimise the chance of an accidental release of toxic gas.
- **Reduce the exposure of people or the environment to the hazard.** For example by ensuring that the factory is not located near to or upwind of centres of population; by providing adequate emergency planning procedures to help in case of an evacuation.

As discussed earlier, the acceptability of a risk has both objective and subjective elements, and the actions proposed to manage the risk may thus be influenced by non-scientific factors, e.g. the degree of credibility and trust between the interested parties. For example, in our chemical factory example, the risk of death from a release of toxic gas may be determined by scientists to be say, 1 in 100,000 per year, which is statistically lower than many other everyday risks, but may still appear too high for certain sectors of the public to accept. Government regulators then have to strike a balance between the extra cost of additional controls to reduce the risk to a more 'acceptable' level, and their 'pay-off' in terms of increased safety. It is here that 'trust' becomes very important, since if the general public (or special interest groups) have little trust in government to determine such a trade-off, people are less likely to accept the regulator's evaluation of the risk, and may continue to call for a higher level of safety or oppose the building of the factory.

3.2.4 Risk Communication

Because of the importance of perception and trust, risk communication has assumed increasing prominence as part of the overall risk management process in recent years. Communication involves exchanging information and ideas between those identifying, evaluating and managing risks and, as suggested in Figure 3.1, can be seen as influencing, and influenced by, each of the other stages in risk assessment. Since subjective judgements, values and perceptions of risk can be so important, many academics, industrialists and regulators now conclude that talking and listening to interested groups and individuals can help in making decisions and increase the likelihood of their acceptance.

While it is generally accepted that communication between the interested parties is an important part of risk assessment, there is less agreement on the best way to communicate. Many attempts at risk communication rely on a 'one-way' process of simply presenting the facts and probabilities to the public; analysts or decision-makers state the risk statistics and may also place them into some sort of context by comparing them with the risks from other activities. For example, the chemical company wishing to build the factory in our example may attempt to gain acceptance of the risks (calculated at say, 1 in 100,000 per year) by comparing them to those from other activities such as those shown in **Table 3.2**.

---

[3] However, HFCs contribute to global warming, so reducing a risk in one area may not reduce the risks in another.

TABLE 3.2 COMPARATIVE RISKS OF DEATH

Activity	Risk of Death per Year
Smoking 10 cigarettes per day	1 in 200
Natural causes at age 40	1 in 700
Coal mining	1 in 7,000
Road accidents	1 in 14,000
Workplace accidents	1 in 50,000
Exposure to nuclear effluents	1 in 70,000
Clothing and footwear manufacturing	1 in 300,000

Source: (22)

Since the risk of death from a road accident is 1 in 14,000 per year, the chemical company might place the risks from the proposed factory 'into perspective' by pointing out that the risks from the factory are much less than from driving a car (which almost everyone finds tolerable for the benefits it brings). However, psychological and social research has shown that this sort of approach has its limitations. As Figure 3.2 showed, people's perceptions of the risks of different activities do not relate directly to calculated risks - so a simple statement that a chemical factory is statistically safer than driving a car may be at best ignored by the general public, or at worst taken as evidence that risk assessors are out of touch with what people really think.

Risk comparisons are most effective when activities are compared which carry similar perceptions of control, dread, timing, etc. For instance, a comparison of the risks from hang-gliding with those from skiing will be given more credibility as both activities are voluntarily undertaken, do not involve catastrophic consequences and are not likely to affect future generations. So, a more useful comparison for the chemical company might be say, with the risks from other industrial activities or effluents.

Research has also shown the importance of how a particular risk message is portrayed, since messages can be easily distorted by media coverage, by interest groups, or through personal attitudes. Examples include media coverage of large-scale transport accidents (such as the Clapham rail crash, motorway pile-ups, or the Herald of Free Enterprise sinking), compared to the normal day-to-day accidents that claim more lives but rarely feature in news stories. This form of distortion (or 'amplification') makes it appear that the risks are greater than the statistics would suggest. The opposite ('attenuation') has the effect that certain activities appear less risky than the statistics show. Examples here include perceptions of the risks of prostate cancer or smoking. For instance, many men are unwilling to be tested for prostate cancer because they may consider it embarrassing, so the disease is perceived to be less widespread than it really is. In the case of smoking, many smokers are aware of the risks involved, but underplay them by either comparing them to the risks of other activities, or believing that they personally have a lower than average risk of lung cancer or heart disease - clearly, however, not all smokers can be at less than the average level of risk.

Research into risk communication in recent years has focused on its role in the decision-making process. As discussed earlier, where an agency has a high degree of credibility, and can be seen to be open and honest in its dealings, the level of trust that people place in its decisions tends to be higher. This has led to suggestions of ways to improve communications (and hence, the degree of trust), which involve extending the scope of decision-making to encourage participation and **two-way communication** involving discourse, co-operation and consensus. This approach involves interested parties **collectively** defining a problem and agreeing a solution (see Box 3.2 in next Section).

Current traditional approaches to resolving conflict (typified by public inquiries) rely more on one-way communication where intentions are announced and then defended, often in adversarial conditions that can alienate those who feel they should be involved (23, 24, 25). At present, the UK planning system involves the greatest degree of participation in decision-making. Local planning authorities have a legal duty to advertise proposed developments, take objections into account and hold a public inquiry if necessary. While this system seeks to be inclusive, some still see it as relying too much on an adversarial legal system, rather than moving towards an open two-way communication (or 'discourse') where positive attempts are made to reach consensus between parties with opposing views (23, 24, 26). Similarly, a public inquiry often limits discussion to considering only a narrow range of possible alternatives to a proposal. For example, under current arrangements, a public inquiry for a proposed new road can only consider alternative routes for the road, but cannot consider more basic alternatives such as rail-based schemes (27). However, in its recent Green Paper on Transport (28), the Government has proposed that decision-making for transport schemes should be broadened to take account of other factors, and aimed at building consensus on regional priorities; such as where the balance should be struck between economic development, quality of life and environmental protection when deciding on new transport schemes.

3.2.5 'Social' Models of Risk Assessment

As discussed earlier, many risk practitioners and researchers argue that risk assessment is not just based on quantitative ('objective') science, but is influenced by judgements, values and perceptions. Moreover, that subjective elements can occur **throughout** an assessment, including the so-called 'scientific' stages of risk identification. The argument continues that, when assessing risks, there must be a balance between psychological perceptions, social and cultural values and scientific/engineering analysis. How easy is it to mesh these two potentially incompatible approaches?

In many areas of risk assessment, quantitative methods have a long track record which is still seen as reliable, comprehensive and acceptable. This is particularly the case in workplace safety, where the conditions may be most favourable for making accurate estimates of risk. As one moves away from simpler situations, however, - e.g. into the area of environmental protection, matters get considerably more complicated and uncertainties start to creep in which can have a substantial effect on the outcome.

In such circumstances, an alternative approach would be to describe the risk in words rather than in numbers. For instance, the professionals involved might characterise the possible risks to health of the chemical factory in our example to be 'significant', just as in recent weeks, the risk of contracting CJD from eating beef has been described as 'extremely small'. These approaches suffer from the weakness, however, that there are no universally accepted definition of a 'significant', 'small', etc. risk, and immediately invite the response 'how big is small?' Also, people may simply not accept the risk irrespective of its size, because of issues such as dread, control, etc. Under such circumstances, professionals involved must have a high degree of credibility and must be trusted if the public is to accept their assessment. A problem faced by government is that scientists from environmental organisations are more likely to be trusted by the public than those from government departments or from industry (15, 16).

As uncertainties become significant in environmental risk assessments, the precautionary principle (PP), becomes more relevant. Here there is still some debate over when it is appropriate to use the principle and how strongly it should be applied (29). For instance, the Third Ministerial Declaration on the North Sea of 1990 required the precautionary principle to be invoked *"even where there is no scientific evidence to prove a causal link between emissions and effects"*, whereas UK environmental policy (5) states that precautionary action will be taken *"where there are significant risks of damage to the environment"* but only *"if the likely balance of costs and benefits justifies it"*.

The PP is an important consideration when dealing with environmental risks for a number of reasons:-

- Firstly, impacts may be unquantifiable because our current understanding of the effects of human activities on ecological systems may be incomplete as data may be unavailable; systems may be too complex to deal with readily; or we do not know or understand all the relevant parts of human and ecological systems or how they might interact.
- Secondly, traditional appraisal methods have limitations, especially where attempts are made to place numerical or monetary values on intangible assets like the environment or quality of life. In cost-benefit analysis, many problems remain in trying to put money values on landscapes or ecologically-sensitive areas, and, discounting long-term costs and benefits to present-year values, effectively emphasise short-term effects.
- Thirdly, there is the danger of wholly unforeseen impacts - for example of DDT on birds' eggs, CFCs on the ozone layer and (a more recent concern) the possible effects of chemical residues on male fertility.

Where such uncertainties make a quantitative risk assessment (QRA) difficult, the precautionary principle can substitute in a number of ways: e.g.

- by setting targets based on best technical (or practicable) means;
- by eliminating the substance concerned;
- by setting arbitrary reduction targets based on political negotiations and subjective judgements.

Whatever approach is adopted, there is the discrete issue of the extent of public participation in the decision-making process. Some (e.g. 6) argue that experts and 'sound science' should be left to make decisions, and others (e.g. 19) argue that science needs to be extended into the civic realm where experts, governments and the public develop a consensus around the inherent uncertainties and tolerable risks to help make acceptable decisions.

Most recently, some approaches are being developed (11, 19, 20, 26, 30-36) which blend attributes from qualitative and quantitative approaches in both the natural and social sciences. While the exact way in which both types of information are brought together may differ (37, 38), the process of decision-making is intended to be:-

- **Open** - the process is transparent to all who wish to review the decisions. Thus, the overall policy framework and all assumptions made and the uncertainties generated are made explicit and are open to debate, and technical information is presented in a clear, unambiguous form suitable for a non-expert audience. An example of this is the statutory requirement for a non-technical summary for an Environmental Statement.
- **Accountable** - those making decisions are responsible for them, and it can be seen where the final decisions are made, and by whom.
- **Credible** - those making decisions can justify them on technical grounds, but also ensure adequate communication takes place between experts, decision-makers and other interested parties based on trust and credibility.
- **Inclusive** - the process avoids being 'captured' by technical experts, as often the perceptions and values of non-experts can provide valuable insights. Thus those with differing values and perceptions, and those who stand to benefit and lose from the decision are included in the process.

Examples of how decisions can be made that go some way to meeting these objectives include lay panels, stakeholder groups, round-table meetings, visioning exercises and Agenda 21 partnerships. While each of these processes has its own particular method, they are all based on making decisions by building consensus, where people with opposing views work together to seek solutions that they can all support, in contrast to the traditional approach relying on decisions being made and announced and then defended against disagreement. This latter 'decide-announce-defend' model often leads to conflict between opposing parties, and debates can lose sight of the underlying issues. This approach can also extend the length of time needed to gain consent, as decision-makers spend a long time trying to 'sell' the idea, and defend against opposition (36).

Seeking a consensus acknowledges that areas of disagreement will exist, but tries to keep discussion on the issues by building trust between interested groups. A consensus-building exercise may use an independent third-party to mediate in areas of disagreement, and to help build the necessary trust and a feeling of collective responsibility in making the decisions. This approach may increase the time spent starting the process and making the decision, however, less time may be needed to 'sell' the idea, because many interested parties will already have been involved in the decision. Indeed, supporters of this approach argue it can result in consent being granted quicker than with the 'decide-announce-defend' model (36). On the other hand, it has to be recognised that the logistics of involving all interests in the consensus process may be very great, and on issues where there is little common ground or fundamentally-held beliefs which lead to opposition in principle, consensus may be difficult, if not impossible, to generate.

The 'consensus' approach is being tried on some policy questions, and a recent example is how Hampshire County Council determined its strategy for waste disposal - described in **Box 3.2**.

BOX 3.2 HAMPSHIRE'S WASTE STRATEGY

Two-fifths of Hampshire's waste is currently disposed of by incineration, but under tighter environmental standards, four older incinerators will have to close during 1996. However, the main currently available alternative is to dispose to landfill, but there are not enough sites available in the county. As a solution to this problem, the County Council decided and announced that a single larger incinerator should replace the four older ones. Local opposition to the scheme was intense, and after two years of defending its proposal, the Council abandoned the idea.

However, the basic waste disposal problem remained, and since traditional 'decide-announce-defend' approach had not worked, the Council decided to try using a consensus-building approach to find a widely acceptable solution. The Council and interested parties worked together to examine the underlying causes of the county's waste problem, and from this a waste management strategy was developed. Following widespread telephone interviews with local people, three advisory lay panels were set up to represent the interests of people across the county. Both technical information and people's values were considered, so communication of the issues was two-way - with the Council both informing people of the underlying problems, but also listening to what local people had to say. The Council also kept people informed on the progress towards a solution, and the advisory panels were provided with technical information and help to interpret it, so the scientific issues could be understood and the panels could make realistic suggestions.

Finally, a set of recommendations was agreed, and the resulting consensus was that although waste-to-energy incineration was one of the least favoured options, it was better than taking the waste out of the county for disposal. The Council has, therefore, now achieved a more widespread sense of agreement on the way forward, and as many of the interested parties were actively involved in the consensus-building, there is a greater sense that they have participated in making the decision, and they are more likely to trust the judgements of those making the final choices.
Source: (23, 39)

3.3 Risk Assessment in Government

As already mentioned, much of today's legislation and regulation is aimed at decreasing risks to people or the environment, and the main principles involved in risk assessment are therefore germane to all government departments. This section thus looks at how risk assessment is applied across departments and recent measures to bring some central direction to the question.

3.3.1 The Current Uses of Risk Assessment

Risk assessment has evolved to different degrees in different departments in response to a range of threats to public safety and the environment. The first attempt to take stock of who did what and why in this field was in 1992 when the Interdepartmental Liaison Group on Risk Assessment (ILGRA) was established - an informal forum for officials from all government departments and the Health and Safety Executive (HSE) with responsibility for policy development and practical application of risk assessment. ILGRA was convened to discuss risk assessment issues and to explore the extent to which a common approach could be developed. The group produced a report at the beginning of 1996 that looked at how risk assessment is currently used across departments, focusing on its use in the protection of health, safety and the environment (40). In its report, ILGRA noted that, while risk assessment is simple in principle, it is more difficult in practice because risk is *"an uncertain mixture of science and policy"* spanning many disciplines, including engineering, natural sciences and social sciences.

ILGRA noted that each department had evolved its own approach to using risk assessment, according to its historical traditions and its main objectives, and the group found a wide variation in how risk assessment is currently used to support decision-making. Overall, risk assessment plays a role in many government functions (outlined in **Table 3.3**), and is applied in many departments, as summarised in **Table 3.4**.

TABLE 3.3 RISK ASSESSMENT IN GOVERNMENT

Function	Application	Example
Investment	Setting public spending priorities.	Deciding overall budgets and balancing expenditure between policy areas.
Regulation	Balancing risks and benefits of regulations.	Setting appropriate safety levels for chemicals: e.g. sales bans or precaution notices.
Enforcement	Optimising enforcement efficiency.	Identifying targets for enforcement, and setting the appropriate frequency of inspections, etc.
Education	Advice on general health and safety issues.	Guidance on work place health and safety risk assessment and food preparation.

Source: (40)

TABLE 3.4 HOW RISK ASSESSMENT IS USED IN GOVERNMENT

Department	Approach and Application
Transport	Quantitative methods for safety standards for roads, vehicles, aircraft and railways often based on historical accident statistics.
Home Office	Mainly in fire safety and emergency planning. Also used to assess likelihood of reoffending or absconding.
Forestry Commission	Compliance with health and safety legislation.
Inland Revenue	Limited use in information technology.
MAFF	Qualitative and quantitative methods for food safety, pesticides, veterinary medicines, genetically-modified organisms, flood defence, fisheries, conservation.
Customs and Excise	Some quantitative methods for enforcement priorities and resource deployment.
Scottish Office	Qualitative and quantitative methods for assessing environmental effects of planning applications.
Welsh Office	Pollution incidents and contaminated land remediation.
Defence	Quantitative methods for safety designs, radiation dose, explosives deployment, weapons procurement, environmental protection and health and safety.
Health	Qualitative methods for safety of medicines, food safety, air and water quality standards, emergency planning, vaccination and immunisation strategy assessment of medical devices and health promotion.
Education & Employment	No formal methods, but informal analysis for refining and informing decision-making.
Trade & Industry	Qualitative and quantitative methods for consumer safety, impacts on small firms, work programming, insurance company reviews, oil and gas regulation and decommissioning of facilities.
Environment	Qualitative and quantitative methods for radioactive waste disposal control of chemicals, pollution prevention and control, global atmosphere changes, land use planning, contaminated land control, waste management, habitat protection.
Health & Safety Executive	Qualitative and quantitative methods for resource allocation, enforcement of health and safety legislation, standards setting, decisions on tolerability of risks.

Source: (40)

While there was broad agreement on the objectives of risk assessment, the group accepted this did not mean that all departments should adopt exactly the same methods. Nevertheless, it saw scope for harmonisation and recommended that departments should :-

- Achieve greater coherence and consistency within and between departments.
- Facilitate inter-departmental co-operation on risk issues.
- Improve Government's communication with the public on risk matters.

There are also underway some trials on new approaches to risk assessment, exploring the consensus approach discussed above. One project (total value £57,800) sponsored by the Department of Trade and Industry (DTI) and carried out through the Energy Technology Support Unit (ETSU) has the aim of deriving a new approach to planning renewable energy schemes (41). Procedures which involve consensus-building are being tested for use as part of the formal planning process. The project will report on the feasibility of adapting existing procedures, gaining local involvement, and using interactive computer networks and CD-ROMs to provide information on policy, planning procedures, local guidance and technical data. One output of the project will be a guide for developers on the steps necessary to gain planning permission, the groups they should contact, and when the consultation should take place. Also, the guide will be of use to local authorities in helping them make their decisions, and to local communities by setting out a clear framework for their input to consultations.

3.3.2　　Risk and Deregulation

Regulations, though motivated by the objective of protecting the public, workers, or the environment, can impose significant costs (especially to small businesses), restrict the freedom of the individual and, where carried too far, can stifle innovation, so damaging the economy. It has been a tenet of Government policy (42) in recent years that regulations may have gone too far in some sectors and the Deregulation Initiative was set up to ensure that regulations are proportionate to the problems they seek to control. Following a recommendation of the Deregulation Task Force (DTF) the Government decided that, from September 1995, formal 'Regulatory Appraisals' should be carried out to decide, in the first instance, whether a problem requires regulation, and secondly to match any ensuing regulations to the scale of the problems involved.

Regulatory Appraisals aim to ensure that the costs and benefits of any regulation are balanced. A **Compliance Cost Assessment (CCA)** estimates the **costs** incurred by business and other sectors of the economy of the proposed regulation. **Benefits** are to be estimated on the basis of a **risk assessment**. Regulatory appraisals must be carried out for all regulatory proposals that may affect businesses, voluntary organisations and charities, and Ministers must personally 'sign off' both the CCAs and the risk assessments to certify that the balance between costs and benefits in the proposal is appropriate. To help departments undertake the appraisals, the Cabinet Office's Deregulation Unit issued guidance on undertaking CCAs (43) and risk assessments (44) early in 1996.

As described in **Box 3.3,** the guidance includes advice on how risk assessments should be carried out and advises that the relative benefits of different options for regulation should be judged by how effective they are in reducing risks. The guidance requires these benefits to be valued in monetary terms, and compared against costs to business (determined from the results of the CCAs), consumers and government. Finally, the guidance suggests that the decision whether or not to regulate should also take into account issues of equity and political considerations, such as how fairly the costs and benefits are distributed.

BOX 3.3 THE DEREGULATION UNIT'S GUIDANCE ON REGULATORY APPRAISAL

As part of the Deregulation Initiative, all proposals for regulation must be subjected to a formal Regulatory Appraisal, comprising a Compliance Cost Assessment (CCA) to determine costs to business from complying with the new regulations, a risk assessment to quantify as far as possible the benefits of regulation, and a comparison of costs and benefits, to ensure that the measures proposed are proportionate to the problems identified. The stages necessary are summarised in the Figure, and described in more detail below

FIGURE STEPS IN REGULATORY APPRAISAL

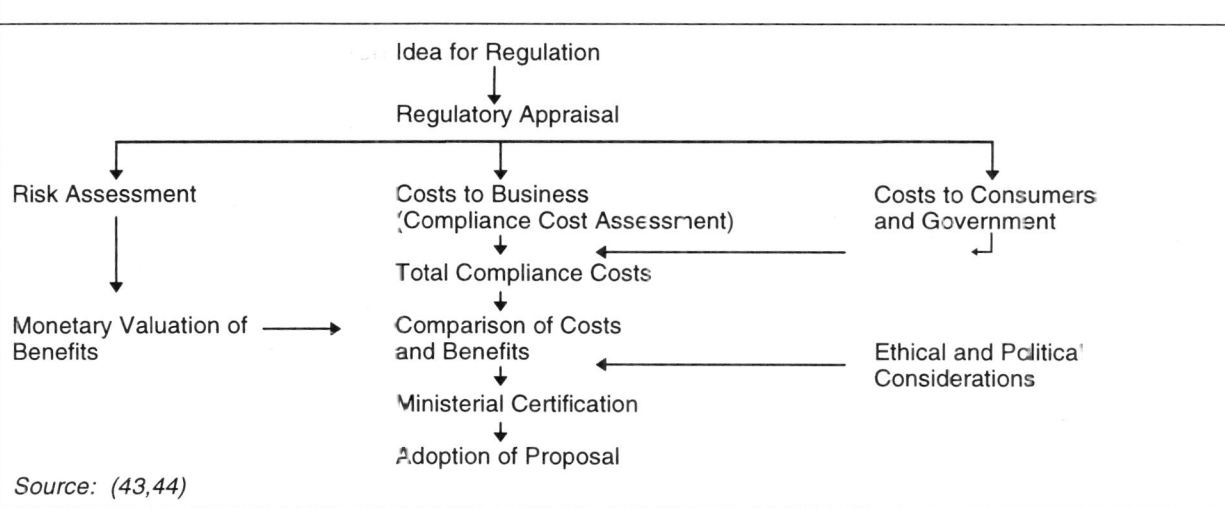

Source: (43,44)

1   Compliance Cost Assessment

Guidance on the CCA element of the Regulatory Appraisal (43) suggests that departments should follow the following steps:

- Outline the purpose of the proposed measure and its intended effects.
- Identify the compliance costs for "a typical business", including any costs that cannot be quantified, key effects on international competitiveness, and monitoring and review arrangements.
- State the types of business likely to be affected and estimate the number of businesses involved (making clear the sources of information and the consultations held).
- Identify the compliance costs for the specific business sectors identified.
- Consider specifically the likely effects on small businesses, voluntary organisations and charities.
- Combine the estimated compliance costs for all specific sectors likely to be affected into an overall statement of likely total annual and one-off costs.

2   Risk Assessment

This comprises four stages:-

(i)   **Identify the problem and the harm.** The situations leading to undesirable outcomes, and those being harmed should be identified. (ii)   **Estimate the risk.** Since this may not be straightforward, estimates are acceptable - either a 'best' or 'expected' estimate based on mathematical expectations, or expert judgements, or best available science (but not 'perceived risk').

(iii)   **Identify options.** A wide range of options to deal with the problem should be considered (including the do-nothing or do-minimum options). Options may include eliminating the risk through outright bans on activities or substances, or changing practice to reduce the risk. Non-regulatory options should be examined, such as voluntary codes of practice or providing information and advice.

(iv)   **Estimate the impact of the options on the risk.**

3   Monetary Valuation of the Benefits of Each Option

The guidance suggests that monetary values should be attached to the benefits of each option where possible, and that where these are likely to occur in the future, they should be expressed as present-year values by discounting. The guidance recognises that attaching monetary values may not be straightforward, especially in areas such as health and environment, where these factors are not traded as 'commodities' with well-defined market prices. In this case, benefits should be expressed in some other quantitative terms where possible, although more qualitative statements such as impacts being 'low', 'moderate', or 'high' may be acceptable.

4   Compare the Costs with the Benefits

For each option, the benefits should be compared against the costs to business consumers and to the government. A net value for the difference between the costs and the benefits should then be determined, or where there are large uncertainties, a range of likely values.

5   Issues of Equity or Political Considerations

Further considerations include issues of **equity** (such as the distribution of benefits and costs) and other political issues. Finally, any divergence between the public's perception of risks and the experts' estimates should be identified, but the guidance emphasises that "*the extent to which they are taken into account when reaching policy decisions should be a matter for explicit ministerial judgement.*"

While the guidance is clear in principle, the complexities and uncertainties of risk assessment discussed earlier create many problems of implementation, including:-

- Placing monetary values on risks and benefits is often difficult and, in the environmental field, subjective. How, for instance, does one assign monetary values to a cleaner atmosphere or an ecologically important meadow? In contrast, costs of implementation will always be expressed in monetary terms. The guidance recognises this, and suggests that qualitative categories can also be used (e.g. assigning risks to 'low', 'moderate', or 'high' categories). The effect of this approach will be that the Regulatory Appraisal may have to weigh, say a risk described qualitatively as 'moderate', against costs with precise monetary values. In common with guidance elsewhere (e.g. 12) the guidance does not explain how such quantitative/qualitative decisions can be made.

- One approach suggested in the guidance is to only justify action when risks are judged to be 'serious'. This term is, however, subjective, and there can be wide disagreement on how seriousness is judged. The wider picture of risk assessment described earlier in Section 3.2, showed how a problem's seriousness can be evaluated by taking account of public perceptions and values to determine what levels of risk would be politically and socially acceptable. Compared to this broad picture, the guidance moves directly from identifying to managing risks- effectively missing out the risk evaluation stage in the assessment process.

- The public's perceptions of risk may differ from those of the experts according to a range of factors such as the degree of control felt by people over the risks; the degree of dread felt about possible outcomes, etc. (see Section 3.2). As well as the complexities and uncertainties involved in some quantitative 'scientific' risk assessments, perception can be very important. The guidance limits the extent to which public perception is taken into account when reaching policy decisions to explicit ministerial judgement, but gives no advice on how such perceptions should be measured to help inform this judgement.

- One aspect of the uncertainties and complexities involved in risk assessment is the possibility that unforeseen risks might occur. Although the guidance recognises that assessing risks involves a great deal of uncertainty, it implicitly assumes that all risks can be identified and quantified, and gives no advice on how to deal with the possibility of unforeseen risks.

- The costs and benefits of any regulation may not occur immediately, but may be delayed until some time in the future. The guidance suggests that people prefer to receive benefits in the short-term, but pay costs in the long-term, and so suggests that discounting be used to reduce future costs and benefits to present-year values so they can be assessed on a common basis. Discounting reduces future values, and thus places emphasis on short-term costs rather than long-term benefits.

Overall, therefore, Regulatory Appraisals seek to incorporate some of the guiding principles of risk assessment described in Sections 3.1 and 3.2, when striking the appropriate balance between the costs and benefits of regulation. It was explained earlier that risk assessment comprises three main stages (identification, evaluation and management of risks), and all stages are made easier by effective communication. In comparison to this picture, the Deregulation Unit's guidance uses the term 'risk assessment' more narrowly; concentrating on quantifying costs and benefits more along the lines of a traditional cost-benefit analysis.

In this context, practitioners recognise that cost benefit analysis (CBA) does not include **all** costs and benefits, and those that cannot be priced accurately (such as some environmental and social factors), are often omitted from the analysis. There has been much debate recently about how these **'external'** costs can be priced and brought within any CBA system, and numerous attempts have been made to do this. Despite this, uncertainties remain and a great deal of debate continues on all sides as to how these problems should be addressed. In particular, questions remain over the practical usefulness of CBAs; how balanced they can be in providing a truly 'objective' picture of the risks and benefits; and the extent to which they are accepted by lay people as a legitimate way of making decisions (45, 46). We return to this matter in Section 4.

3.4   Assessing Environmental Risks: Some Current Practice

Previous sections have described the background to the Environment Agency, outlined the approaches to environmental protection adopted by Agency's predecesssors, and discussed the general principles of risk assessment. This section looks briefly at how risks to the environment are assessed in the specific areas of :-
- Managing radioactive wastes.
- Preventing and controlling pollution.
- Protecting against floods.
- Managing municipal and industrial wastes.
- Controlling contaminated land.

3.4.1   Managing Radioactive Wastes

When deciding its policy on **radioactive waste management,** the Government takes advice from 5 separate bodies: the Radioactive Waste Management Advisory Committee (RWMAC); the Advisory Committee on the Safety of Nuclear Installations (ACSNI); Ionising Radiations Advisory Committee (IRAC); the National Radiological Protection Board (NRPB); and the Committee on Medical Aspects of Radiation in the Environment (COMARE).

While policy is set centrally, regulation is the responsibility of the Environment Agency in England and Wales, SEPA in Scotland, and the Alkali and Radiochemical Inspectorate (ARCI) in Northern Ireland. Government policy is that radioactive waste risk assessment and management should follow the same basic principles applying in other fields (including consideration of sustainable development (47)), and therefore that the risks from radioactive wastes should be reduced to levels comparable to risks accepted elsewhere in society. Radioactive waste management thus involves weighing costs against benefits, and there will be a point where additional costs of further safety improvements exceed the benefits.

To help consider where the balance between costs and benefits might lie, and what risks would be considered acceptable, radioactive wastes are managed according to the principle of the **Tolerability of Risk**, (or ToR framework) which is based on three premises (48):-
- Firstly, there is a level below which society considers the risk from a hazard to be insignificant or broadly acceptable.
- Secondly, there is a level above which the risks are intolerable.
- Thirdly, between these two extremes, risks are tolerable, and action must be taken to reduce them 'as far as reasonably practicable' (ALARP).

FIGURE 3.3   THE TOLERABILITY OF RISK FRAMEWORK

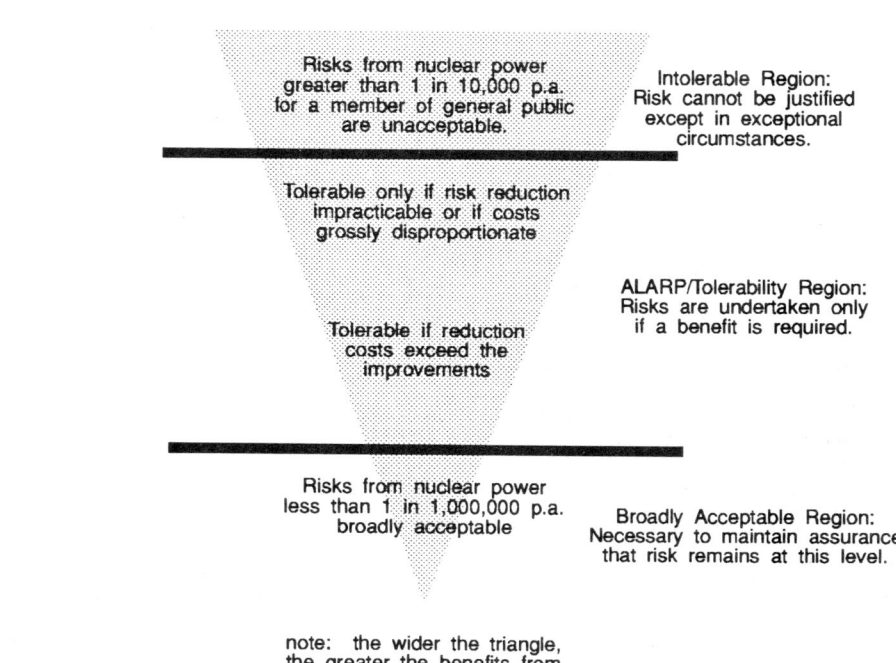

Risks from nuclear power greater than 1 in 10,000 p.a. for a member of general public are unacceptable.

Intolerable Region: Risk cannot be justified except in exceptional circumstances.

Tolerable only if risk reduction impracticable or if costs grossly disproportionate

ALARP/Tolerability Region: Risks are undertaken only if a benefit is required.

Tolerable if reduction costs exceed the improvements

Risks from nuclear power less than 1 in 1,000,000 p.a. broadly acceptable

Broadly Acceptable Region: Necessary to maintain assurance that risk remains at this level.

note: the wider the triangle, the greater the benefits from reducing risks relative to the costs

Source: (44)

This is illustrated in **Figure 3.3**, together with the figures HSE suggest should apply in the case of nuclear power (although HSE now considers the ToR framework applicable to all technological and industrial risks).   Under this scheme, risks are considered intolerable and must be reduced if they are greater than 1 in 10,000 per year for an individual member of the general public (and 1 in 1,000 per year for individual workers), but risks are considered broadly acceptable if they are lower than 1 in 1,000,000 per year for any individual, and no further action to reduce such risks would be needed.   Between these values, risks are not acceptable but may be 'tolerated', provided action is taken to reduce them according to the

ALARP principle. Here, the benefits of reducing risks are compared to the costs, and measures are taken which reduce risks to the lowest level achievable without incurring grossly disproportionate costs. Under ALARP, the costs to benefits ratio which would be considered 'grossly disproportionate' increases as the level of risk increases. This means that (all other things being equal), greater costs would be justified in reducing a risk of 1 in 20,000 than a risk of 1 in 50,000.

Turning to the specific question of radioactive waste disposal, UK Nirex Ltd is proposing to build a deep underground repository, designed to keep the wastes separated from the environment for many tens of thousands of years using a series of artificial and natural barriers (**Figure 3.4**). The waste would be sealed in concrete and secured in steel containers, and these would be placed in a vault deep underground which would be backfilled with cement. This system is based on using a series of engineered and natural barriers so that the maximum risk of death to people at the surface who are exposed to any radiation ultimately emanating from the repository is no more than 1 in 1,000,000 (per year)[4].

FIGURE 3.4 THE PRINCIPLE OF RADIOACTIVE WASTE DISPOSAL

surface

additional rock layers above vaults

undisturbed rock

cement backfill in disposal vault

waste in sealed containers

n.b. not to scale

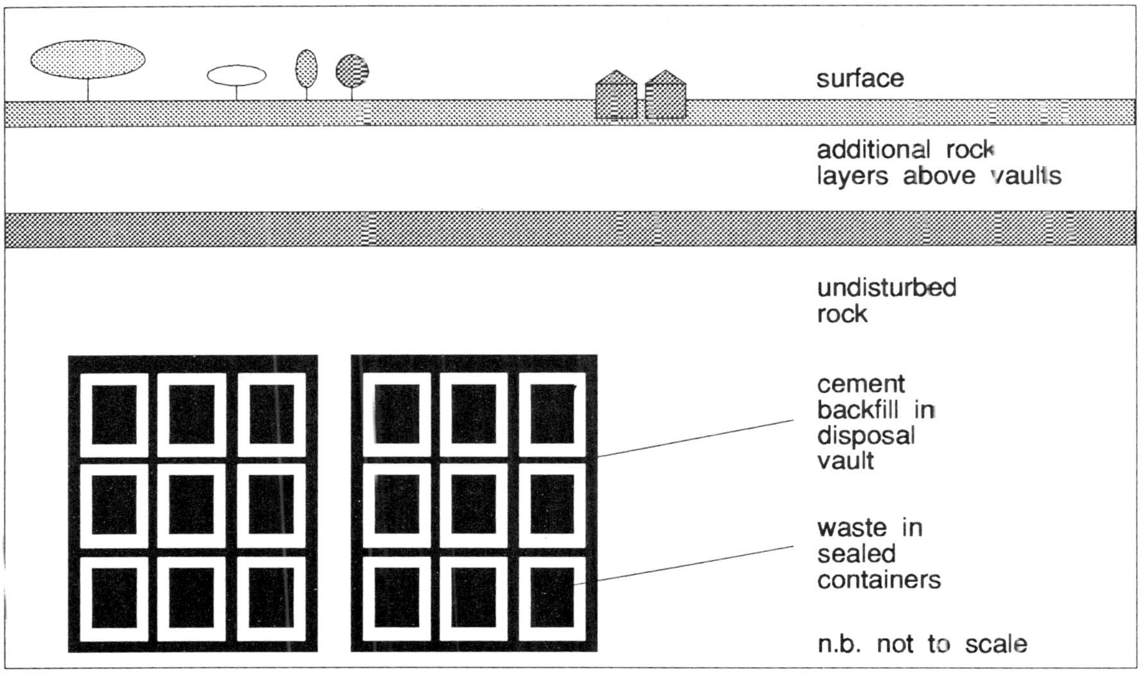

Source: UK Nirex Ltd

The overall risk figure is derived from combining the estimated risks of radioactive material moving across each barrier in succession over the very long timescales considered. For instance, some of the radioactive substances are expected to move from the waste, through the sealed containers into the cement backfill in about a hundred years, and then over the next ten thousand to a million years to migrate out of the repository itself, into the surrounding rock. From there, the probability of small amounts reaching the surface have been estimated and their potential effects on humans calculated - whether through direct exposure or via food or water.

---

[4] However, recent policy (47) has suggested that this risk could be exceeded if the costs of meeting it were 'disproportionate'.

Although conceptually straightforward, assessing the risk at each stage involves complex chemical, physical, engineering and geological calculations requiring large quantities of information on everything ranging from the chemical form of each radionuclide, how they leach into different types of water, the rate at which radioactivity declines through natural decay, the porosity of geological strata, hydrogeology, etc. Nirex's initial estimates persuaded the company that risks are likely to be acceptably low and it is proposing that a Rock Characterisation Facility be built to test out its assumptions and collect information essential to the final risk assessment and repository design proposals.

Nirex's methodology has been reviewed by the Royal Society (49), but because so many stages are present in the risk assessment, there is considerable scope for technical and policy debate and challenge at every stage, and environmental groups such as Greenpeace have focused many of their challenges on such grounds. In such areas, the aspects of risk communication and public acceptance are, in many observer's eyes, becoming as important than the actual methods used in the engineering calculations.

3.4.2 Preventing and Controlling Pollution

Pollution of air, land and water are inextricably linked - for instance sulphur dioxide from a power station can cause damage to lakes and seas through the formation of acid rain; and solid wastes in a landfill can leach pollutants into groundwater and affect water supplies. Recognising these links back as far as 1976, the RCEP introduced the concept of **integrated pollution control** (IPC) (50), where it proposed that industrial pollution should be controlled so that damage to the **environment as a whole** would be kept to a minimum. In 1990, the Environmental Protection Act put this theme on a statutory basis, and HMIP was given the responsibility for applying IPC to the most potentially polluting industrial processes.

Under this regime, risk assessment is seen as useful in improving regulation by defining standards for environmental protection that closely relate to acceptable levels of harm to the environment. Thus IPC's primary objective is to **prevent** releases of potentially harmful substances, but where these cannot be prevented, releases to air, water and land should be reduced to a minimum so that they can cause little or no harm. IPC requires that the procedures used to prevent and control releases to the environment represent the **Best Practicable Environmental Option** (BPEO), and the methods adopted in using the BPEO are the **Best Available Techniques Not Entailing Excessive Cost** (BATNEEC) (51). It is worth noting that BATNEEC does not rely only on technological solutions, but also includes other techniques such as operating environmental management systems, and ensuring adequate staff training. Therefore, the concepts of BPEO and BATNEEC can be seen as a form of environmental protection standard, controlling the basic approach to pollution prevention and control.

The RCEP first coined the term BPEO in 1976 (50), and described it in more detail in 1988 (2). According to the RCEP's definitions, the process of BPEO identifies an industrial process that provides the most benefit (or least damage) to the environment as a whole, at an acceptable cost in both the long and short terms. The process of selecting a BPEO comprises the following basic steps:-
• Defining the objective of the project.

- Identifying options.
- Evaluating advantages and disadvantages of each option.
- Examining the economic and financial costs of each option.
- Summarising and presenting the information to assist in decision-making.
- Reviewing the preferred option to ensure all risks have been considered.
- Monitoring to determine whether assumptions in the design were correct.

A key feature of the BPEO approach is that the decision-making process should be transparent, and that an **'audit trail'** should exist so all stages in the choice of the BPEO can be scrutinised; making all the assumptions and uncertainties in the process explicit.

In an attempt to make the BPEO process more quantitative and consistent, HMIP have developed the **Integrated Environmental Index** (IEI), as described in **Box 3.4**.

BOX 3.4 THE INTEGRATED ENVIRONMENTAL INDEX

A key element in identifying the Best Practicable Environmental Option (BPEO) for a process is to determine the impact of releases on the environment as a whole. However, assessing impacts in an integrated way is complex, and depends on many factors including:
- the amount of each substance released;
- the rate at which substances are released;
- the chemical and physical characteristics and location of releases;
- how easily substances can move between air, water and 'and;
- how much of the released substance already exists;
- the location of targets and their sensitivity to single or mixtures of substances.

As precise knowledge about these factors is not available, HMIP developed a system designed to 'quantify' their assessment of environmental impacts to help judge whether the proposed controls are proportional to the problems identified. The **Integrated Environmental Index** (IEI) is thus meant to provide a measure of the impacts of all substances released into air, water and land (52).

The method is based on comparing the concentrations of substances in the environment, and assessing how significant these are. To do this HMIP developed a set of criteria known as Environmental Assessment Levels (EALs) which provided a numerical basis for analysis. EALs were set in two ways:
- Firstly by adopting specific statutory Environmental Quality Standards (EQSs) laid down under national, European or international law which define the maximum allowable concentrations of certain substances in the environment. For example, the EAL for mercury in inland waters was set at 1 µg/l, as defined by the Surface Waters (Dangerous Substances)(Classification) Regulations 1989.
- Secondly, since statutory standards have not been set for many substances, HMIP developed their own criteria as interim standards, until EQSs are set. For example, HMIP derived many of the EALs for substances released into the air from standards laid down under health and safety law for protecting the people in the work-place, such as Occupational Exposure Limits (OELs).

Having defined the EALs, the significance of the likely pollutant releases can be assessed. Here, the amount of pollution likely to be released is calculated, and added to existing levels to derive a predicted environmental concentration (PEC). The significance of the release is then determined by considering how close the PEC would be to the EAL - defined as the ratio of the two terms (known as the Environmental Quotient, EQ). Where the EQ is more than 0.8 (i.e. the PEC is more than 80% of the EAL), the release is considered significant. and becomes a priority for control.

The method then requires that EQs are calculated for each substance released into each medium and these are added together to calculate the IEI (as illustrated in the Table below). Where two options are analysed and IEIs calculated for each, the option with the lowest IEI (Option 2 in the table) would be the Best Environmental Option (BEO). Where the costs of implementing this are not disproportionate to their benefits, this would be BPEO.

Box 3.4 cont'd.		
TABLE EXAMPLE OF USING IEI TO DETERMINE THE BPEO		
Medium	IEI for Option 1	IEI for Option 2
Air	0.1	0.3
Water	0.3	0.2
Land	0.4	0.1
Overall IEI	0.8	0.6

HMIP regarded the IEI as a simple means of helping to make the choice of the BPEO more transparent, rather than as a prescriptive method that would identify the BPEO precisely and unequivocally. Nevertheless, the method has been criticised by industry and pressure groups on a number of counts (53), for instance:

- Interactions between pollutants in different media are not accounted for;
- Short-term effects are not considered adequately;
- Over-reliance on a small number of numerical indices to represent complex situations;
- Emphasis on dilution rather than elimination of risks.

While HMIP was responsible for authorising individual industrial processes, it did not have a general remit to protect the wider environment, and so responsibility for the **control of water pollution** was given to the NRA under the 1989 Water Act (54). The legislation meant that discharges of pollutants to streams, rivers, lakes, estuaries and coastal waters were illegal unless the NRA granted a 'consent', and these consents served two purposes:

- To enforce the law by placing obligations on dischargers.
- To set limits within which the discharge must stay to avoid harm to the receiving waters.

Consents were based on limiting discharges so that they were environmentally acceptable - i.e. the same as defining a 'tolerable risk', but without specifying the risks in numerical terms (e.g. 1 in 10,000, etc). In many cases, discharges were controlled on the basis of qualitative criteria. Risks were assessed using professional judgement to determine whether the effects of a discharge would be 'significant' or not, and consents based on general descriptions of the types of discharge that would be allowed, or process controls that would be required. Where larger and potentially more harmful discharges were involved, a more quantitative assessment of the risks was used, based on finding out what the environment could absorb safely (the 'assimilative capacity'), and then setting discharge limits so that the pollutants discharged did not exceed the assimilative capacity.

One might illustrate this approach by the example of protecting migrating salmon which are, among other things, susceptible to copper pollution. In **Figure 3.5**, the maximum acceptable level is 5µg/l (based on toxicology), while ambient concentrations are 3µg/l - giving an assimilative capacity of 2µg/l. Having defined the assimilative capacity of the estuary, a sewage works could be permitted to discharge copper as long as the concentration in the estuary after dilution was no more than 2µg/l.

This example illustrates how the NRA's and HMIP's approaches to pollution control differed. Under IPC, HMIP aimed to prevent or minimise releases as a first priority, and then used BATNEEC to implement the most practicable options for pollution control - in effect limiting releases according to what best techniques could practicably achieve at the time.[5]   On the other hand, the NRA had no such overriding prevention objective, and the consents system allowed discharges limited according to how much pollution the environment could absorb.

FIGURE 3.5   THE ASSIMILATIVE CAPACITY APPROACH TO WATER POLLUTION CONTROL

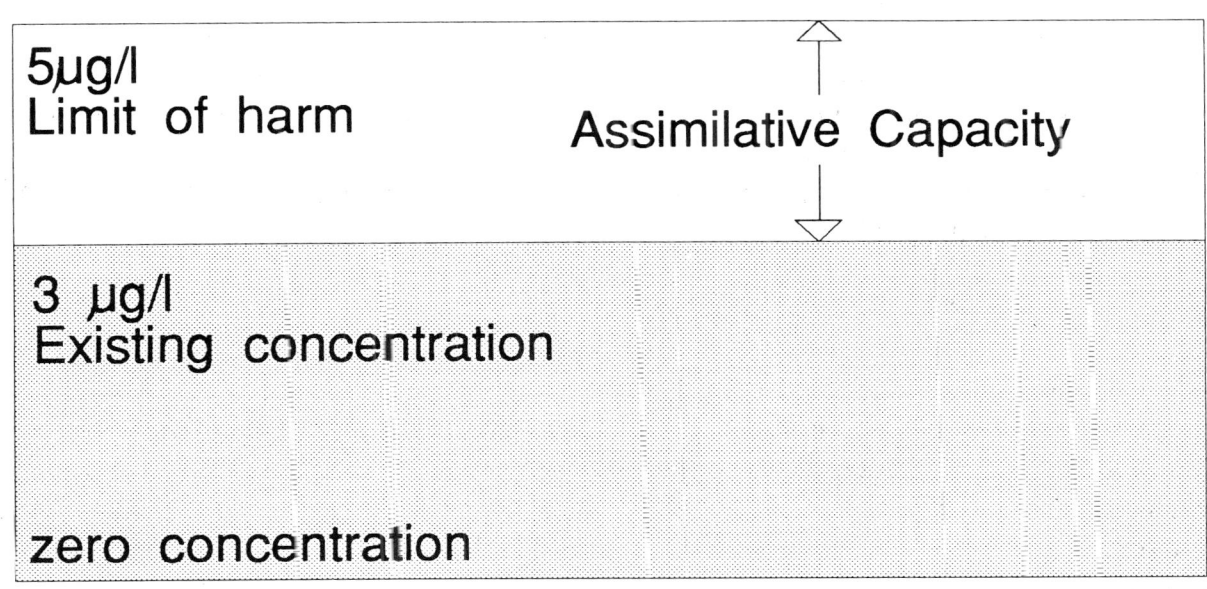

This discussion has concentrated on how risks to the environment from pollution are handled, but HMIP also use risk assessment to help improve its own **efficiency in enforcing regulations** (55).   Historically, HMIP Inspectors used their professional judgement to assess the comparative risks of different processes, and to set priorities for enforcement effort, but more recently there has been increasing pressure to make these judgements more explicit. HMIP therefore developed the system known as **Operator and Pollution Risk Appraisal (OPRA)** which scores numerically how well an operator controls a process, and attempts to rank the pollution risks involved. Under this scheme, the basic scores are multiplied by weighting factors that reflect how important HMIP consider each factor, and the weighted scores added together to produce final ratings for the operator performance and pollution risks. These ratings are then used to decide how often a process needed to be inspected - those with low ratings for operator performance and high ratings for pollution risk are clearly inspected most often.

By using numbers to make the Inspectors' judgements more explicit, OPRA lays down an auditable trail to simplify scrutiny of decisions on enforcement measures. For example, an HMIP Inspector might visit a tannery and note, amongst other things, that the staff were not aware of environmental legislation affecting their operations and that their control of hazardous chemicals on site was inadequate. The Inspector would, therefore, give a low score for operator performance and a high score for pollution risk, and thus recommend that the tannery be inspected more frequently, until its performance improved.

---

[5] BATNEEC was, however, continually under review, and where innovations allowed, standards were improved.

OPRA was still in its infancy at the point that HMIP entered the Environment Agency, and the Agency is expected to develop it further to improve Inspectors' effectiveness and efficiency. Some perceived shortcomings which may be addressed include:-

- Questions over how statistically valid the method is (e.g. if the same (or different) Inspectors examine the same process on different occasions would they come up with the same scores each time?).
- Limitations from using numbers as substitutes for subjective value judgements.
- Questions over how statistically valid it is to combine the scores and weightings.
- Dangers that too much emphasis on the numbers generated may obscure the underlying judgements and uncertainties.
- The judgements of the Inspector under OPRA take no account of the perceptions and values held by the public.

3.4.3   Protecting Against Floods

As well as managing risks to the environment from human activities, the NRA was also responsible for some 43,000 km of flood protection works in England and Wales, accounting for the NRA's largest area of spending. Continuing this into the Environment Agency, means that flood protection will also be the Agency's largest area of spending, totalling some £260M for 1996/7. To decide on the best use of these large sums of money, the NRA has to decide where the priorities are for building or maintaining flood defences, and to do this uses quantitative methods of risk assessment to determine how often storms or floods are likely, and to focus resources on areas most at risk.

The NRA also assesses the engineering requirements for flood defences and conducts economic, environmental and social impact assessments to determine the appropriate balance of costs and benefits. In deciding where it is most cost-effective to spend money on flood defences, the NRA applies a principle of meeting specific 'levels of service', where the use of land at risk of flooding defines how often flooding can be tolerated (56). For example, high-grade agricultural land next to a river might be guarded against flooding, say every 3 years, but a town might be expected to tolerate a flood less frequently, say every 20 years.

3.4.4   Managing Municipal and Industrial Wastes

Following the separation of the regulatory and operational aspects of waste regulation (under the 1990 Environmental Protection Act), the 87 WRAs in England and Wales were given the duty of licensing **waste management** facilities, including municipal and industrial landfill sites, waste transfer stations and waste treatment plants (57, 58). The prime objectives of waste management licences are to prevent risks of pollution of the environment, harm to human health and detriment to local amenities. There is however, an overriding strategy for managing wastes that establishes a hierarchy of options (59, 60). As a first principle, the hierarchy seeks to eliminate the production of waste, along the lines of IPC. Where wastes cannot be eliminated, they should be minimised as far as practicable, and reused or recycled where possible. Only when these other options have been exhausted, should wastes be allowed to be disposed of by incineration or to landfill.

Some, (e.g. Greenpeace) have criticised this approach as the hierarchy itself can be overriden by applying the BPEO approach. Also, it is argued that the waste heirarchy neither takes account of the risks of cumulative impacts nor the potential benefits to be gained from waste reduction or recycling. In addition, current guidance on waste management licensing (57) does not require an explicit assessment of the risks to the environment, human health or amenity. However, risk assessments are legally required under the 1994 Waste Management Licensing Regulations, and so can help WRAs identify which waste facilities and which operators may be the most 'risky', and so help WRAs to set appropriate conditions on licences in accordance with the waste management hierarchy. The legislation requires that persons holding licences are "*fit and proper*" and the guidance gives detailed advice on how the WRAs should determine whether applicants meet this condition (e.g. by checking applicants' criminal records). Also the WRAs must check the technical competence of operators and monitor the licensed facilities.

Perhaps the most explicit form of risk assessment in general waste licensing is where an applicant is required to make financial provision to cover the costs of possible clean-up action in the event of harm being caused, and to set aside sufficient funds to cover the costs of rehabilitating and monitoring the site once it has closed. The guidance suggests that this provision should depend on the "*capabilities for pollution and harm*" of facilities, but does not set out any specific guidance as to how these risks should be assessed.

Although there is no central guidance on assessing risks for general waste management licences, the DoE provides more specific guidance to WRAs on the design, construction and operation of landfill sites (58) - i.e. the last available option in the waste management hierarchy. This guidance acknowledges that all landfills will leak pollutants to some extent, and so suggests that the risks of harm caused by the leakage should be calculated, and the design should be modified until the risks are acceptable. The DoE and NRA have developed a risk assessment tool called LandSim to support the guidance, and this will be released officially by the Agency later this year.

As an example, as illustrated in **Figure 3.6**, water in a landfill might leach mercury from batteries in household waste, and this pollutant could then leak through the landfill liners, move through soil and rocks to an underground water supply, where it could be pumped to the surface and enter drinking water, presenting possible risks to health.

Such quantitative risk assessments become the basis for the design and operation of the landfill. The main weakness of this approach is that the guidance is based on a presumption that all potential risks *can* be identified and described quantitatively, and takes no account of the possibility of unforeseen effects; nor does it suggest how the uncertainties inherent in any risk assessment should be dealt with. Similarly, there is no recognition of the importance of public perceptions of risk as discussed earlier. For instance, local inhabitants might be more worried about landfill gas, litter, odour and traffic from the site, than about possible contamination of water supplies. In this case, they may call for proportionally more resources to be allocated to controlling those risks they perceive to be the most threatening, rather than accepting the priorities preferred by the WRA or industry.

FIGURE 3.6 SOME RISKS FROM LANDFILLED WASTE

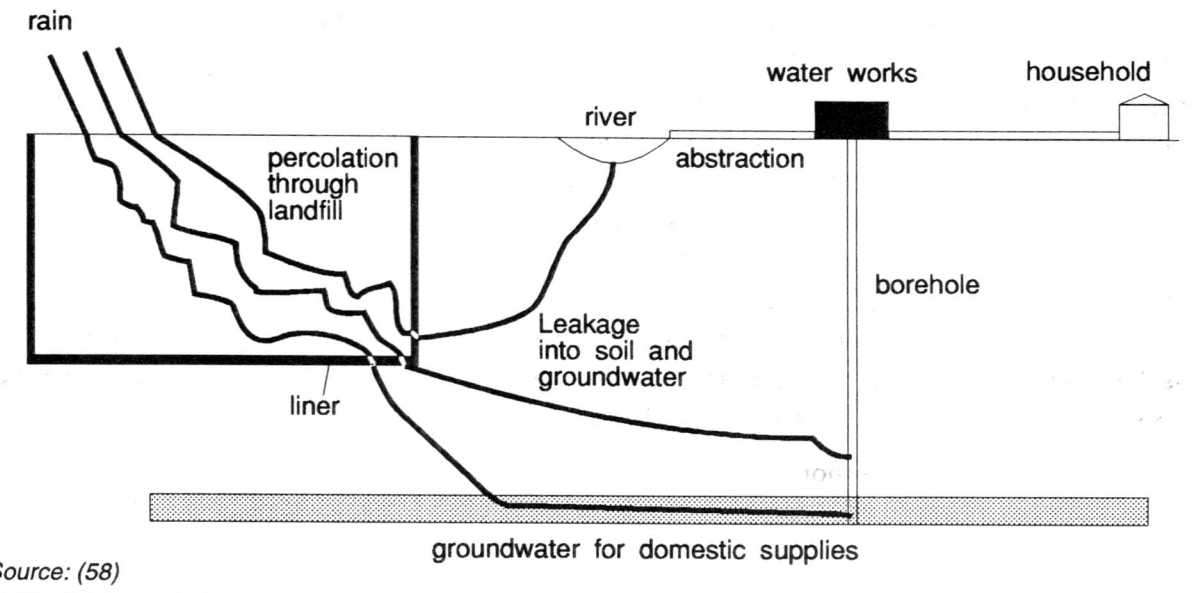

Source: (58)

3.4.5   Controlling Contaminated Land

POST has previously reviewed the control of **contaminated land** (4) and, in summary, the system applies guidelines and standards on acceptable levels of contamination in soil set by the Interdepartmental Committee on the Redevelopment of Contaminated Land (ICRCL). The ICRCL guidelines were based on the principle that risk is related, *inter alia*, to the use of land - thus guideline levels for acceptable levels of contamination in gardens or allotments would be lower than for land under concrete such as car parks or offices. Examples of risks from contaminated land are given in **Table 3.5**, a fuller listing is given in POST's previous report (4).

TABLE 3.5 SOME RISKS FROM CONTAMINATED LAND

Contaminant	Sources	Risks
Toxic metals, e.g. mercury, lead, arsenic, copper, cadmium.	Metal mines, steel works, foundries, smelters, scrap yards, sewage works, paint factories.	Damage to health due to toxicity.
Inorganic compounds, e.g. cyanides, acids, alkalis.	Plating works, gas works, chemical factories.	Damage to buildings from chemical attack; Damage to health due to toxicity, corrosive action or skin irritation.
Organic compounds, e.g. coal tar, phenols, oils, solvents, chlorinated compounds.	Gas works, dye factories, pharmaceutical industries, oil refineries, petrol stations, dry cleaning.	Damage to health due to toxicity, corrosive action skin irritation, and may be carcinogenic.

Source: (4)

Policy on contaminated land has some similarities to the ToR framework discussed earlier. Concentrations of contaminants in soil below a certain 'threshold trigger level' mean that soil can be treated as though it was not contaminated (this corresponds to the level of broadly acceptable or insignificant risks in the ToR framework). Levels of contaminants above an 'action trigger level' mean that some remediation **must** be carried out - corresponding to levels of unacceptable risk in the ToR framework. Between the two extremes, there is an area of 'tolerable' risk, and for contaminated land, the DoE recommend that professional judgement should be used to assess how significant risks might be, and to decide on the best course of action.

While the ICRCL standards have been widely used, they have been criticised by many including the House of Commons Environment Committee (61), which recommended that the DoE should derive a range of quality objectives and guidelines for different classes of land. More recently, the Welsh Development Agency, supported by DoE, have developed a set of risk-based guideline levels to replace the ICRCL criteria, and the Environment Agency has been given the responsibility for producing a national strategy for contaminated land in conjunction with local authorities. To help the Agency in drawing up the strategy, the Government will produce statutory guidance later this year setting out how contaminated land should be defined and identified. Also, the guidance will describe who should be liable for harm resulting from contamination, and how the costs of cleaning up contaminated sites should be paid for. At present, however, questions remain over how the risk assessment principles described earlier will be used in defining and assessing 'significant' contamination and harm, and how subjective judgements, perceptions and values can work alongside the traditionally 'scientific' approach.

3.4.6   General Themes in Assessing Environmental Risks

The above discussion outlined how environmental risks have been assessed in the past by different bodies under different regulatory regimes, and this comprises the starting point from which risks will be assessed and managed for environmental protection in the future. But how consistent have the approaches been in the different fields? Similarities and differences in the approaches taken are highlighted in **Table 3.6**.

Overall, the main **similarities** are that most environmental risks have been assessed using quantitative approaches based on identifying tolerable levels of risk; social aspects such as risk perception and communication have largely been secondary factors. The basic approaches have thus focused on predicting how pollutants move through the environment and what effects they may have on different targets (e.g. effects on human health through contamination of drinking water or reductions in air quality, or effects on the ecology of a river through the build-up of heavy metals). From these calculations, most methods rely on standards, guidelines and professional judgements to decide what levels of risk will be acceptable or unacceptable. Only the ToR framework specifies the risks involved numerically as probabilities, such as 1 in 10,000 per year.

The main **differences** between the approaches were that IPC and waste management licensing were based on a 'prevention first' philosophy, where the parent legislation set down an overriding objective to prevent releases of pollutants, or the production of waste, as a first priority. The other functions had no such overriding objective, and were based on allowing discharges, but only up to a certain level based on an assessment of the harm caused. For instance, discharge consents were set according to the assimilative capacity of receiving waters, and flood protection standards were set according to a frequency of flooding considered to be appropriate for a particular land use.

TABLE 3.6 HOW ENVIRONMENTAL RISKS WERE ASSESSED

Environmental Protection Function	Responsible Authority Prior to Environment Agency	Method of Risk Assess-ment	Basis of Risk Assessment	Comments
Control of Radioactive Waste	HMIP	Quantitative	Tolerability of Risk (ToR) framework - i.e. minimise risks between predefined acceptable and unacceptable levels.	ALARP principle used to ensure that more effort put in to reducing greater risks.
Integrated Pollution Control	HMIP	Quantitative	Integrated Environmental Index (IEI) - similar to ToR, but risks not specified.	Overriding requirement to prevent releases as a first priority. Also use of EALs may not equate to HSE's use of ToR.
Protection of Water Quality (Discharge Consents)	NRA	Quantitative	Assimilative capacity - i.e. discharge up to levels the environment can absorb.	No overriding requirement to prevent releases as a first priority.
		Qualitative	Professional judgement of risks.	Used mainly for small discharges.
Flood Protection	NRA	Quantitative	Levels of service appropriate for different land uses.	Approach similar to ToR, as relies on agreeing tolerable risks of flooding.
Waste Management	WRAs	Quantitative	Professional judgement of acceptability of calculated risks.	Used for landfill design, but should prevent pollution and harm.
		Qualitative	Identification of "fit and proper persons".	Overriding objective to prevent waste production. Risks implicit on criminal record, technical competence and financial provisions of applicants.
Control of Contaminated Land	DoE	Quantitative	ICRCL trigger levels based on different land uses.	Similar to ToR, but professional judgement used in range of tolerable risks. Acceptable and unacceptable levels of risk not made explicit.

The approaches used by the Agency's predecessors also need to be placed in the context of guidance from the DoE on risk assessment and management for environmental protection (12). This guidance is summarised in **Box 3.5** and goes some way further than the traditional approaches to risk assessment used by the Agency's predecessors, exhibiting some features common to the broader picture of risk assessment discussed earlier in Section 3.2.5. In particular, the DoE sets out what science can tell us of how the environment functions, but recognises the inherent uncertainties and limitations in that knowledge. Furthermore, the DoE notes that risk assessment is and always will be judgmental to some extent, and that the process needs to be iterative, taking account of the less tangible factors such as perceptions and quality of life issues which affect what levels of risk (if any) are acceptable or tolerable, and so help define the most appropriate risk management measures.

BOX 3.5 DOE GUIDANCE ON RISK ASSESSMENT AND MANAGEMENT

In June 1995, the DoE published its guide to the use of risk assessment and risk management for environmental protection (12). The guide explores some of the underlying principles of risk, and is aimed at generalist readers, policy makers and managers who need to ensure they can set guidelines for a risk assessment and can critically appraise what is presented to them. The guide discusses how risks (especially environmental risks) are assessed and managed in a systematic way as a contribution to the UK's sustainable development strategy, published in 1994 (7), where it stated that "*decisions should be based on the best possible scientific information and analysis of risks.*" In this context, the DoE's guide suggests that the commitment to sustainable development is a principal reason for performing risk assessment and risk management.

The guide acknowledges that decisions often have to be taken on the basis of incomplete information and sometimes in circumstances of significant uncertainty, and in this context, the guide cautions against being misled by formal risk assessments into thinking that the quantification of risks (especially in areas of great uncertainty) are more accurate than they really are. When potential damage is uncertain and may be significant, it is necessary to act on the precautionary principle (see also Box 2.1), and risk assessment has a role to play in deciding when to apply the principle.

In the DoE's guide, '**risk assessment**' is taken to include the estimation and evaluation of risks (i.e. their magnitude and significance), and '**risk management**' is the process of implementing decisions about accepting or altering risks, based on balancing the costs and benefits of possible actions. The guide sets out the five stages leading up to risk estimation (describing the intention; identifying the hazard; identifying the consequences; estimating the magnitude of consequences; and estimating the probability of consequences) and considers how the magnitude and probability of consequences can be brought together in an assessment of the risk. Further, it discusses how risks should be evaluated, taking into account factors such as risk perception, confidence in the overall process, issues such as 'quality of life' or 'environmental quality', and whether there are any over-riding requirements to meet minimum standards. The guide then expands its earlier discussion of the precautionary principle and how it can help achieve sustainable development, and finally discusses how environmental monitoring programmes should be established and how they fit into the risk management process.

The principal points brought out in the guide are that:

- Even though risk estimation may include subjective judgements, there is considerable value in even attempting to describe an intention and its possible consequences.
- Achieving sustainable development is a principal aim of risk evaluation, but the precautionary principle should be used only where hazards have long environmental lifetimes or accumulative or irreversible consequences - especially when there is considerable uncertainty as to the link between the hazard and the consequence.
- Risk perceptions depend on a wide variety of factors, such as the degree of dread, control, familiarity, etc., and so independent expert assessors can be a useful means of achieving objectivity.
- Risk assessment will lead to risk management decisions that reflect priorities that have been assigned to various parameters, including the less tangible factors such as perception, quality of life, etc. In this context, it can be difficult even to agree on a definition of the environment or on what constitutes 'damage' or 'harm'. For instance, are the loss of non-renewable resources and genetic diversity always harmful?; should there be an overriding need to preserve human life at any cost?; is the intention to protect human health, buildings, ecosystems, associations of species, individual species, populations of a given species or individual plants and animals?
- Given the breadth of potential impacts, it may not be easy to decide where an environmental risk assessment should start.
- Irrespective of the risk assessment and cost benefit analysis, any intention may be subject to an overriding requirement such as ALARP, BPEO or BATNEEC.
- Risk management is inevitably part of the iterative process and should inform any monitoring system which should be tailored to the affected environment and be able to reduce uncertainty about the consequences of actions.

One further theme is **how far risks are used as the basis for setting environmental standards**, since historically, standards have been set to protect a range of targets from a variety of hazards. For example, HSE sets standards that control airborne pollutants in the workplace, while DoE sets standards for the protection of the health of the general public or for protection of ecosystems. Some environmental standards (e.g. the concentration of nitrogen dioxide in ambient air) are defined by statutory requirements often stemming from EU Directives; others (e.g. levels of nitric acid) do not have such legal backing and are derived from other sources, such as occupational exposure limits.

In this context, it is clear that there is no uniform logical link between the level of risk involved and the standard set - even in procedural terms. The ToR framework developed by HSE for nuclear power stations does employ 'tolerable' and 'acceptable' risk figures to set standards for radiological protection. On the other hand, standards set to stay within the 'assimilative capacity' of the environment, do not generally make the levels of risk of environmental harm explicit. Neither do many other standards (e.g. ambient air quality standards) relate these to a specific target risk.

Practice thus often blurs the distinction between the various conceptually separate stages in risk assessment and management. Thus, when the Expert Panel on Air Quality Standards (EPAQS) recommended its standard of 50 $\mu g/m^3$ for fine particulates (PM10), it did not make explicit what level of risk it had considered acceptable. Equally, scientific advice on the BSE issue made recommendations on operational matters (e.g. witholding of certain tissues from the food chain) on the basis of the Expert Committee's 'judgement'. Of course there are good practical reasons for this, often arising from the inherent difficulties of quantifying the risks involved. Nevertheless, there are concerns that inconsistencies in approach may leave society with distorted priorities in its expenditures on health and safety. This complex area is currently the subject of an inquiry by the RCEP, and the findings are expected to be published by the end of 1996.

We return to these topics again in the next Section, and consider how the Environment Agency might deal with some of its future challenges in using risk assessment, particularly in integrating its current practices within the framework of sustainable development.

4.1   Why is Risk Assessment Important?

Even with much effort to express this subject in everyday terms, the description in the previous section will appear abstract and arcane to many. It is thus worth reminding ourselves why RA is important in a society where a primary role seen by the electorate for Government is to protect against risks ranging from collapsing buildings, sinking ferries, environmental disasters and even the minutest threat to health. Risk Assessment is basically an attempt to bring consistency to this complex web of interacting pressures in order to achieve:-

- **equity** - the sense that all should have similar 'rights' to protection;
- **value for money** - in the sense that society's resources for health, environmental etc. protection are finite, and it thus makes sense to allocate these according to their relative importance.

But is the present system achieving these objectives? The answer has to be no if two illustrations are relevant. First, let us consider risks to health from radioactivity in its various forms. **Figure 4.1** shows how the risks from various sources vary, from present day risks of 1 in 2,000 (per annum) if one lives in some houses in radon-rich parts of the UK, to planning for 1 in a million risks in thousands of years time where the final disposal of radioactive wastes is concerned. Not only do the 'risks' to individuals vary by a factor of 1,000, but it is difficult to argue that public perceptions of threat or pressures on expenditure reflect these calculated risks.

FIGURE 4.1   RISKS FROM RADIOACTIVITY

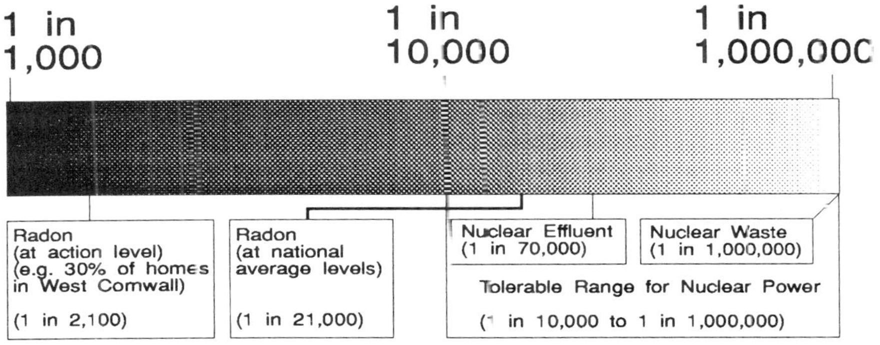

| 1 in 1,000 | 1 in 10,000 | 1 in 1,000,000 |

Radon (at action level) (e.g. 30% of homes in West Cornwall) (1 in 2,100)

Radon (at national average levels) (1 in 21,000)

Nuclear Effluent (1 in 70,000)

Nuclear Waste (1 in 1,000,000)

Tolerable Range for Nuclear Power (1 in 10,000 to 1 in 1,000,000)

Source: NRPB

Risk assessments can also help quantify whether value for money is being obtained in regulations relative to other uses to which that money could be put. If one considers the expenditures on coastal sewage treatment mandated by the EC Bathing Waters Directive, a risk assessment (62) suggests the main health benefit is a reduction in an already low risk of gastroenteric and ear infections - perhaps avoiding tens or at most hundreds of such cases each year. Would such limited outcomes be seen as good value for several billions of pounds if spent via the Department of Health? Of course, such analyses do not indicate that it is it wrong to clean up discharges to sea, but it does show the scope for substantial variations in value for money, where risk assessment can inform the debate about priorities across different sectors.

4.2   Strengths and Weaknesses of Risk Assessment Methods

If risk assessment has an important role, Section 3 discussed how it is applied. To recap, the process of assessing risks comprises the following elements:
- **Risk Identification** - where the chances of particular outcomes of proposals are identified and quantified (where possible).
- **Risk Evaluation** - where the social and political acceptability of risks are assessed.
- **Risk Management** - where the original proposals are adapted to prevent or reduce risks to a tolerable level.
- **Risk Communication** - where information and ideas are exchanged between interested parties.

Each of these is inter-related (as shown in Figure 3.1 on page 10), and each element has its own strengths and weaknesses, summarised in **Table 4.1**. The main strength is that, in its ideal form, the risk assessment process can be used to make decisions in a structured and systematic way, making the many assumptions, value judgements and uncertainties involved more explicit. The main weakness is that the process relies on experts being able to identify and quantify all relevant risks, even though understanding of the complexity of human and environmental systems is not complete. There is thus a danger that the 'precise' figures from a risk assessment will mislead people into thinking they are more reliable and certain than they really are.

TABLE 4.1   STRENGTHS AND WEAKNESSES OF QUANTITATIVE RISK ASSESSMENT

Element	Strengths	Weaknesses
Identification	Allows reduction of problem into component parts for ease of analysis, and can help make assumptions and judgements explicit.	Knowledge and understanding of complex systems is not complete; reduction into component parts can miss factors that affect the system as a whole. Some risks cannot be quantified in the first place.
Evaluation	Allows potentially complex analyses to be expressed in simple probability terms, that can be used to decide between competing priorities.	Simple statements of probability can mask hidden factors, and too much reliance may be put on the numerical outputs, without adequate consideration of the underlying assumptions and uncertainties.
Management	Allows measures to be identified that maintain risks at 'tolerable' levels. (e.g. ToR framework)	The process can be undermined by failure to account for uncertainties, perceptions and values, especially where decision-makers are little trusted to make fair trade-offs. Also relies on their being levels of risk that would be acceptable or tolerable.
Communication	Can simplify discussion to deal only with relative probabilities and to educate the public about the assessment process.	Top-down, one-way communication fails to account properly for psychological and cultural aspects of risk, and is often added-on at the end of the 'scientific' analysis to help in 'educating' the public.

As risk management has moved from the arena of controlling obvious hazards (e.g. grossly visible pollutants such as smoke or obvious toxins such as lead) to more subtle effects at low levels of exposure (e.g. radioactivity, pesticide residues), two things have happened. Firstly, the actual scientific challenge to identify and quantify the risk has grown, together with the uncertainties involved; but secondly, the general concern of the public over unquantified threats to health and the environment has also increased. Such concerns may not be greatly influenced by whether the calculated risk of a pollutant is 1 in a million or 1 in 10 million, but may be greatly influenced by one particular well-publicised event, or by a well-orchestrated public campaign. Consequently, the scientific evaluation of a risk's importance and the public perception can differ widely.

These trends mean that risk assessment can no longer be regarded **exclusively** as an exercise of the traditional 'natural' sciences (i.e. physics, chemistry, biology and engineering), with experts communicating to the public to explain how the risks were calculated. 'Risk' also has social and psychological aspects, while even the 'scientific' aspects of a risk assessment have subjective elements in many cases (63-70), as shown in **Table 4.2**.

TABLE 4.2 SUBJECTIVITY IN RISK ASSESSSMENT

Element	Application of Subjective Judgement
Identification	What questions to ask in the first place.
	The methods chosen to answer the questions.
	Assumptions, simplifications and value judgements used in answering the questions.
Evaluation	What levels of risk are acceptable, tolerable and unacceptable.
Management	Where the balance is struck between costs and benefits of risk management options.
Communication	How far public perceptions and values are included in the assessment.
	The methods and language used to communicate.
	How much information is released and how it is communicated.
	The extent of participation in decision-making.

Recognising a problem is one thing; doing something better is quite another, and a debate has been raging for some time between those who argue that decisions must be based on the best quantitative assessment of 'objective risk', and those who claim that there is no such thing, and all concepts of risk are subjective. The DoE's guidance on risk assessment (described in Section 3.4.6) moves some way to recognising that, particularly in the environmental field, data shortages and uncertainties make many quantitative risk assessments difficult. The DoE thus recognises a need to integrate matters of perception into the process throughout.

One possible model of risk assessment is thus to see experts not as delivering the ultimate quantitative verdict on a particular risk, but as **informing rather than dictating**, risk management decisions. This could involve bringing together the skills of the natural scientists in determining the risks themselves, and those of social scientists in helping to improve public involvement and communication during the risk assessment process, and in helping the public to establish what levels of risk are acceptable.

Section 3.2.5 described some attempts to integrate public perceptions throughout and developed a more consensual approach. While such exercises may well be successful locally, many argue that national methods of risk assessment should not move too far from their scientific basis, and the emphasis should be on social science helping in the process to help develop a more acceptable outcome, rather than becoming the dominant influence on the standards or regulations themselves. Indeed, the Government has chosen not to build on the DoE's recognition of the role of perception, preferring to keep its emphasis in guidance to the Agency (see next Section) on *"sound science"*.

A key lesson of research into perceptions of risk (Section 3.2.5) is to emphasise the **importance of gaining and maintaining trust and credibility for decision-makers, regulators and industry** in order to gain public acceptance (or even support) for proposals. Research by CERM at the University of East Anglia (16) (see **Figure 4.2**) has found that fewer than 20% of people trust advice on environmental risks given by government (7.6%), companies (12.8%) and the media (16%), but over 75% of people trust doctors (76%), environmental organisations (80%), friends (80%), and family (87.2%).

FIGURE 4.2 TRUST IN INSTITUTIONS

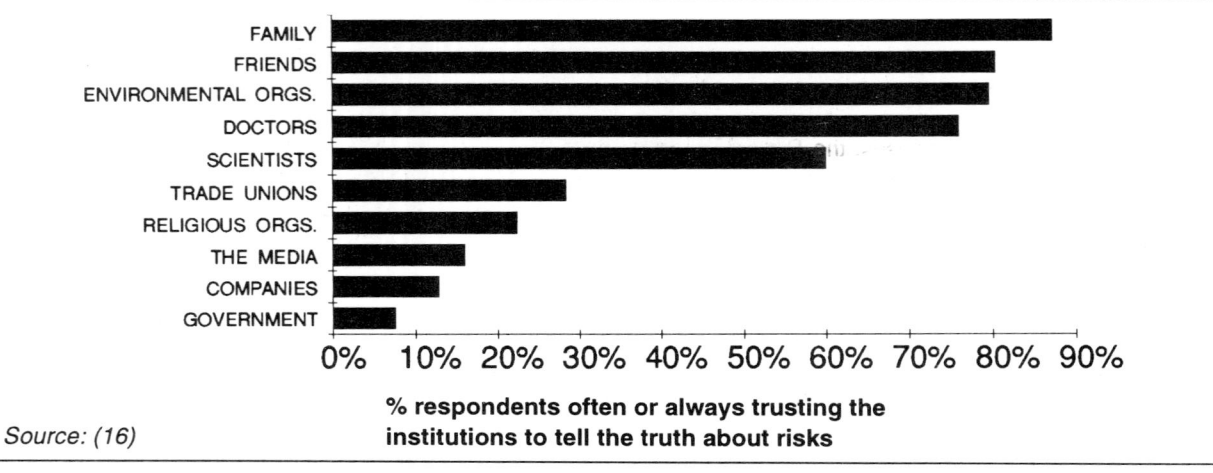

Source: (16)

% respondents often or always trusting the institutions to tell the truth about risks

Other areas of risk research suggest general principles which might be incorporated into risk assessment procedures. For instance, the scope of consultations could be broadened to include:-

- early consideration of proposed developments; taking account of all likely alternatives (including the option to do nothing);
- wider participation to identify and include public perceptions and values.

On the first of these, there is growing pressure for **alternatives to a project** to be considered more comprehensively, and the revised EC Environmental Assessment Directive will make this a statutory requirement in the near future. Such measures might help avoid the criticism that traditional consultations tend to restrict the scope of discussion (e.g. public inquiries into road schemes are restricted to considering only alternative routes for the road), so that broader participation could tackle questions of fundamental policy, such as how transport needs should best be met (e.g. through the 'Great Transport' debate). Turning to more specific **options for broadening public participation,** on a general level these include consensus conferences, round-table advisory groups, and Local Agenda 21 partnerships (see **Box 4.1**).

As discussed in Section 3.3.2, however, the guidance emanating from the Deregulation Initiative is tending to restrict rather than broaden considerations in risk assessment. Thus the guidance ties the process to **'objective'** risk assessment and leaves any consideration of perception to Ministers. Equally, the emphasis on costs moves the process much closer to a narrow cost-benefit analysis. In this respect, the latest proposals **are in the opposite direction to that favoured by much risk research.** We examine this in the context of environmental risk in the next section.

BOX 4.1 METHODS OF ENCOURAGING PARTICIPATION

Consensus conferences emerged in the late 1970s in Denmark as a way of encouraging local and regional debate on promoting Danish economic life. They aim to involve ordinary citizens from widely differing backgrounds is assessing topics of technological and scientific interest, and to include the moral, ethical and personal perspectives of the 'non-expert' (71). Consensus conferences not only to stimulate public debate, but also give valuable feedback to decision-makers on people's attitudes and perceptions, and highlight contentious issues. Essentially, the conference is a forum in which a group of lay people put questions about a controversial scientific or technological issue to experts, listen to their answers, reach a consensus among themselves, and then report that consensus to a press conference.

As part of its strategy to implement sustainable development, the Government set up the **UK Round Table on Sustainable Development** to build consensus between different sectors of society (72). The main purpose of the Round Table is to encourage discussion on major issues of sustainable development between people approaching the topic from widely differing positions, covering a wide range of responsibilities. Where it is not possible to establish a consensus, the Round Table will seek to reduce the differences and clarify the issues. The Round Table is co-chaired by the Secretary of State for the Environment and Professor Sir Richard Southwood FRS. There are a further 30 members, drawn from high-level people from industry, local government, academia, trace unions, environmental organisations, and independent research bodies. In its first year of working (1995), the Round Table met 5 times, and covered issues related to transport, energy and mechanisms for environmental management.

At the United Nations Conference on Environment and Development (UNCED) in June 1992, Member States adopted **Agenda 21** - an action plan to guide national and international implementation of sustainable development (73). Agenda 21 makes it clear that all sectors of society need to work together and that most local authorities should have consulted with their local populations to achieve a consensus on a 'Local Agenda 21' by the end of 1996. Most Local Agenda 21 initiatives are guided by a steering group comprising of a wide range of members of the community as well as local authorities. However, most of the work is carried out by small working groups liaising with already established community groups and official agencies so that Local Agenda 21 does not duplicate their effort, but acts as a focus for local initiatives and places them in the context of sustainable development. Government guidance requires that the Environment Agency "*should seek to make a full contribution to initiatives under Local Agenda 21*".

4.3   Risk Assessment Methods in the New Agency

4.3.1   The New Agency

The Environment Agency faces many challenges in bringing together responsibilities which range from flood defence to nuclear waste, and targets for protection which range from human health, through land and property, to the diversity of ecosystems. There are a number of immediate challenges which arise from the need to blend together the approaches to risk assessment inherited from its constituent parts, but perhaps more importantly, a number of more strategic questions related to developing a longer term strategy.

4.3.2   Short Term Issues

4.3.2.1   The Philosophy of Environmental Protection

The Agency has been formed from three distinct and separate organisations, each with its own approach to protecting the environment. These approaches were reviewed in Section 3.4, and a number of similarities and differences noted in Table 3.6. The main differences in approach were that HMIP and the WRAs operated under a regulatory regime that required releases and wastes to be prevented as a first priority; - where these could not be prevented, they should be minimised and rendered harmless. On the other hand, the NRA had no such overriding 'prevention first' principle, and issued consents for discharges to water based on the 'assimilative capacity' of the receiving waters.

These differences may appear greater than they are. In practice, prevention is limited in both technical and economic terms, and through the principles of BPEO and BATNEEC, HMIP (and the WRAs) recognised that prevention was not always practicably possible. The main emphasis has thus been on regulating emissions to avoid or minimise harm to the environment through appropriate emission standards and other controls. Equally, the 'assimilative capacity' approach can be limited. In some cases, where the assimilative capacity is already exceeded, the environment can hardly accept additional inputs of pollutants, and an alternative basis of control has to be used. In other cases, our understanding of the particular pollutant involved, its effects on the receiving environment (Section 3.2.1) etc. may be incomplete, and the scientific basis for calculating assimilative capacity thus lacking. In many cases therefore, NRA has had to set emission standards based either on process standards (such as for sewage works) or on the basis of individual negotiations with dischargers. Nevertheless, the Agency has still inherited two different basic philosophies and the question arises **whether the Agency will try and move more widely to a 'prevention first' or 'assimilative capacity' philosophy in all fields of environmental protection.**

In this context, the Government has stated (1) that the principal aim of the Agency is to **protect and enhance the environment as a whole,** and all parts of the Agency now have the necessary powers to prevent or minimise pollution, whether through IPC, the waste management hierarchy or equivalent considerations applying to discharges to water courses. It appears therefore, that the Agency will control pollution and waste under an **overriding objective to prevent releases to air, water and land as a first priority.**

Where wastes cannot be prevented, releases will be permitted, but there will be an onus of proof on the discharger to demonstrate that releases have been minimised as far as practicable, and that they will not harm the environment or human health. In setting standards, regulators will still need to know what levels of pollutants can be tolerated before harm is caused, and thus in practice, the Agency will have to develop a pragmatic way of amalgamating the 'prevention first' and 'assimilative capacity' approaches. In this context, a number of bodies (e.g. the Council for the Preservation of Rural England - CPRE and the National Society for Clean Air and Environmental Protection - NSCA) argue that continued reliance on 'end-of-pipe' technologies should **not detract from the primary importance of developing cleaner production techniques to eliminate or minimise waste** and some (e.g. Greenpeace) go a step further and question the need for some processes (e.g. those that use organochlorine chemicals) in the first place.

4.3.2.2   Deciding the Geographical Boundaries of Control

As described in Section 3.4, the Agency sees HMIP's integrated pollution control and NRA's integrated river basin management (IRBM) as two pillars of its overall strategy to develop a more holistic approach to environmental protection (74). IPC started from a position where HMIP regulated **industrial processes** on a site-specific basis. Now, the Agency wishes to apply the IPC principles over wider geographical areas, such as whole industrial complexes. This could allow a more strategic approach to reducing pollution by setting area-wide targets which would be met by concentrating on those processes contributing the most pollution to an area.

IRBM on the other hand, started from the **river basin** as its **geographical unit,** and was based on reconciling the many conflicting uses to which water was put by setting strategic objectives and targets for environmental quality along specific stretches of rivers, lakes and groundwater zones. It was principally restricted to protecting the water environment, but the Agency plans to extend its scope to deal with other issues including industrial process regulation and waste management.

The process-based IPC is thus extending its geographical area, while the area-based IRBM is extending its coverage to other processes. While both are motivated by a desire to take a strategic view of the environment, care will be needed to avoid duplication or different approaches emerging between those parts of the Agency extending IPC into wider geographical areas, and those extending IRBM to include regulation of industrial process. This raises questions, therefore, of **how the Agency will bring together the aims of IPC and IRBM into a single approach that takes a strategic, long-term view of the environment as a whole.** Indeed, CPRE has called for environmental assessments (EAs) to be carried out on the Agency's plans, programmes and policies on a more strategic level than in the past, where EAs have traditionally been restricted to specific projects (75).

4.3.3 Developing a Longer Term Strategy

4.3.3.1 The Challenge

The short-term problems arising from the merger of different approaches to risk assessment and cultures have also to be set against the background of a number of equally important factors, all of which will need to be brought into play in developing a longer term strategy for the Agency. These include:
- developing a more consistent framework for risk assessment across the Agency's many functions;
- applying lessons from risk research;
- applying the precautionary principle;
- contributing to sustainable development;
- accommodating deregulatory policies.

4.3.3.2 A Consistent Framework

As already mentioned, the Agency brings together previously separate responsibilities for protecting against a number of risks. The breadth of the Agency's responsibilities means that it is responsible for:-
- Risks of very different natures ranging from flooding, through physical and chemical risks to radiological risks.
- Specific targets for protection, ranging from human health, individual animals or plants, to property and agricultural land.
- General targets for protection include survival of species, biodiversity, habitats, etc.

The fact that such a range of functions now reside in one Agency offers the opportunity to apply a more consistent approach than was possible as separate Agencies. Such an approach (Section 4.1) could offer greater equity and value for money if resources can be focused on areas where investment and expenditure will deliver the greatest benefit.

The Agency is already looking at some of the cross-sectoral aspects of its inheritance, and **one option could be to institutionalise a strategic review process** and seek to develop a set of agency-wide standards and guidance which will lead to the most important risks being identified and resources and expenditure redeployed to reflect the new priorities. While one option would be to assign this as a general duty to all operational units, it may be more effective (given the day-to-day preoccupation of operational demands and the inbuilt loyalty to each unit's way of doing things) to **establish on a longer-term basis a central unit charged with developing consistent risk assessment strategies**, targets, valuation methods, etc.- essential if the full benefits of bringing the component parts of the Agency together are to be realised.

4.3.3.3 Applying Lessons from Risk Research

As discussed in Sections 3.2 and 4.2, much risk research suggests that risks should be assessed on a broader basis than hitherto, and attention paid to the more qualitative aspects. For instance, the ways in which different sectors of the public perceive risks, and how these perceptions influence the extent to which risk management decisions are accepted. In addition, even the expert quantitative risk assessments are accepted to often contain some subjective elements, while **the credibility of any agency or organisation is increasingly seen as vital in gaining people's trust in risk management issues**. How do these recent insights into risk affect how the Agency will operate?

Section 3.4 described how the Agency's predecessors assessed environmental risks, and showed that historically the approaches relied mostly on quantitative methods. This approach had the associated danger that the assessment process may be seen by some as 'captured' by experts and decision-makers, and that concentrating on the numbers themselves may obscure the underlying uncertainties, assumptions and complexities. The more recent risk research suggests that public perception is very much influenced by other factors, in particular the degree to which the process of decision-making is:-

- **Open** - the process is transparent to all who wish to review the decision; thus the policy framework assumptions made and the uncertainties generated are made explicit and subject to debate.
- **Accountable** - those making the decision are responsible for it.
- **Credible** - those making the decision can justify that decision based on technical competence, involving both natural and social scientific principles.
- **Inclusive** - the process avoids being 'captured' by technical experts, as very often others have valuable insights that go beyond what science can achieve. Thus those with differing value systems, and those who stand to benefit and lose from the decision are included in the process.

There has been some recognition of these more qualitative aspects by Government, and many departments now consider that risk management is essentially *"an uncertain mix of science and policy"* (43). Also, specific advice on assessing environmental risks from DoE (12,

76) and HMIP (77) has recognised the limitations and (to some extent) subjective nature of scientifically 'objective' risk assessments. Indeed, more specifically, HMIP's guidance recognised the need to take account *"explicitly"* of differing perceptions of relative risks, and saw that openness and the involvement and participation of all interested parties was *"the key"* to the process of risk assessment. In this context, HSE has advocated and used this approach for a number of years in setting limits on exposure to chemicals in the workplace. Here, experts from both within and outside the HSE make recommendations on standards and these are subject to public consultation.

In view of the high degree of scepticism among the public over Government's assessment of risks (Figure 4.2), perceptions of the Agency's own credibility may be influenced by the Agency's relationship to Government. Currently, the Government's draft statutory guidance would require the Agency to operate to *"high professional standards, based on sound science, information and analysis of the environment and of processes which affect it"*, and it may be appropriate to ask if this will prevent the Agency from adapting its policies to **broaden its assessment of risks to take account of subjectivity, public perceptions and values that fall outside of the traditional remit of quantitative methods of risk assessment?**

The Agency considers that realistically, decisions must combine these elements, recognising that 'sound science' can only **inform rather than dictate** a decision (74). Thus, during its first year, the Agency expects that it will continue to use its predecessors' methods, but it hopes to expand the role of the Centre for Integrated Environmental Risk Assessment (CIERA) to include life sciences (covering conservation and biodiversity) and social sciences (covering economics, psychology and sociology) (78, 79). In due course, it is hoped that CIERA will be able to develop new inter-disciplinary approaches to environmental risk assessment, **redefining 'sound science' to combine the principles of the physical, natural and social sciences** (43, 79). Such a trend would be supported by groups such as CPRE and Greenpeace (67,75), who argue that risk assessments must extend beyond 'sound science' and include additional considerations where applicable (such as ethical values, effects on rural communities and the quality of landscape).

4.3.3.4   The Role of the Precautionary Principle

The **precautionary principle** (Section 3.2.5) has been developed in recent years as a specific response to dealing with uncertainties in the field of environmental protection and there is some debate **how far this principle should be applied in policy and decision-making.** Some see the principle as requiring only initial scientific evidence before precautionary action is justified to avoid potentially significant risks. Others (including the UK Government (5) and the House of Lords Sustainable Development Committee (6)) have argued for a more considered interpretation. Thus where the environmental costs of inaction are high and the financial costs of avoiding that risk are low, the precautionary principle should clearly lead to early action. Where environmental risks are low or speculative, and/or costs of avoiding action very high, it may be desirable to consider carefully the balance between costs and benefits or collect more scientific data, before deciding what action to take.

To date the precautionary principle has not been developed into a rigorous system for policy analysis, but it does reflect three important considerations (33):

- **The role of science in decision-making is subject to challenge**, as our understanding of human and ecological systems is uncertain - whether due to the unavailability of data, complexity of systems, or limited knowledge of the relevant interactions in human and ecological systems.
- **Appraisal methods are increasingly recognised as having their own limitations**, especially attempts to place monetary values on environmental assets and quality of life.
- **The extent of public participation in decision-making is now seen as more important, with a role for dialogue** between experts, governments and the public to create consensus around inherent uncertainties and tolerable risks.

How, then, should uncertainties be dealt with when assessing risks? Essentially, there are three options which help to establish the basis of the assessment as 'sound science':-
- **Make the uncertainties explicit** - set out clearly where assumptions have been made and the accuracy of the data used.
- **Calculate how changes in the assumptions used, and the accuracies involved, affect the outcome of the calculations.** Often such a 'sensitivity analysis' can identify where small changes in some factors can alter the outcomes critically.
- **Identify a range of conditions that could exist in the future and examine what might happen if those conditions occurred.** Such a 'scenario planning' approach takes no account of the relative likelihood of each scenario, but establishes plans for each eventuality. In environmental studies, the 'worst case' scenario is often used as the basis for planning, thus ensuring that the most vulnerable are protected. If the 'worst case' scenario is not used, by monitoring how conditions change, plans for different contingencies can be put into effect.

4.3.3.5   *Contributing to Sustainable Development*

Section 2 described how the Agency is also required to contribute towards achieving sustainable development, defined as *"development that meets the needs of the present without compromising the ability of future generations to meet their own needs."* One principle of sustainable development is that there may be a need to take action in the absence of full scientific certainty where the risks of inaction are significant (the precautionary principle), as discussed in the previous Section.

The Government requires that in order to meet the goals of sustainable development, the Agency should:
- Take an **holistic approach** - taking account of the interactions and effects of pollutants discharged into the air, water or land.
- Take a **long-term perspective** - particularly on effects which may be irreversible, or which affect future generations.
- Maintain **biodiversity** - including both sites of nature conservation importance protected by law and non-designated sites which are still important.
- Encourage industry (through partnerships) **to adopt improved technologies and management techniques.**
- Develop **close and responsive relationships** with the public, local authorities, representatives of local communities and regulated businesses.
- Provide **clear and readily accessible advice and information** and become a **recognised centre of knowledge and expertise.**

One of the key aims of sustainable development is to establish **partnerships** between different sectors of society to promote economic development and environmental protection. These partnerships implement Agenda 21 of the Rio Declaration which aims to encourage wider participation in decision-making, recognising the roles to be played by individuals, groups, businesses and governments. Sections 3.2 and 4.2 above described the increasing importance of consensus-based approaches to decision-making; recognising the benefits of a more open, accountable, credible and inclusive decision-making process that takes account of perceptions and values alongside traditional science-based approaches.

The Government requires that the Agency works in *"close and responsive"* relationships with others. Thus, it must establish Statutory Environmental Protection Advisory Committees (SEPACs) and become involved in Local Agenda 21 initiatives. The moves in pursuit of sustainable development thus mesh well with the lessons on risk perception and communication described in Sections 3.2 and 4.2. However, there is some debate over how the Agency, the SEPACs and local authorities can work together in integrating strategic policies, such as over the forthcoming guidance on contaminated land, the National Waste Strategy and the forthcoming National Air Quality Strategy.

These developments suggest that there will be increasing pressure for the Agency to adopt an approach based on wide participation that seeks to include as many views as possible in arriving at broadly acceptable decisions. Indeed, CPRE has called for the guidance to the Agency to make an explicit reference to including non-government organisations and other government departments in the Agency's consultations (75). The question remains, therefore, **how far the Agency will go towards basing its decisions on building consensus among a broader range of interested parties.**

4.3.3.6   *Taking Account of Costs and Deregulation*

The Agency is required to take account of the costs of its decisions, and it must also apply the principles of deregulation to ensure that actions taken are proportionate to the likely harm involved. This may bring into focus the question of **where the balance should be struck between economic development and environmental protection,** as well as between the various sources of guidance on risk assessment emanating from the Deregulation Unit, the DoE and the various approaches in the Agency itself.

The duty to take account of costs was the subject of much debate during the passage of the Environment Bill through Parliament. To clarify many of the points raised in the debates, the Government's guidance to the Agency sets out the scope and purpose of the duty, namely that *"the duty does not apply in cases where it would be unreasonable nor can it be used to override other statutory requirements."* While the exemption for legal obligations (say, in a standard in an EU Directive) is clear enough, the term "unreasonable" is less easy to define, and the Government requires the Agency to develop its own internal guidance on how it will assess the likely costs and benefits of its actions and decisions. One of the main areas of difficulty will be in expressing such costs and benefits in monetary terms, and here the CPRE has called for this guidance to include advice on assessing unquantifiable costs.

Turning now to the Deregulation Initiative, Section 3.3.2 described how government departments are required to undertake Regulatory Appraisals before new regulations are adopted. These appraisals must consider the costs to business, government and consumers of complying with regulations, and balance these against the benefits to be gained (estimated via a formal risk assessment). Although the general principle of the guidance on Regulatory Appraisal is clear, the earlier discussion highlighted a number of potential problems in its implementation:

- Placing monetary values on risks and benefits is often difficult and, in the environmental field, can be very subjective.
- Judgements of when risks are "serious" are subjective, and can be a source of wide disagreement.
- The public's perceptions of risk may differ from those of the experts. Such considerations are reserved for *"explicit ministerial judgement"*.
- One aspect of the uncertainties and complexities involved in risk assessment is the possibility that unforeseen risks might occur.
- Discounting places more emphasis on short-term costs than long-term benefits.

A further issue is that government guidance takes no account of the possibility that **costs to one business sector may be benefits to another**. The environmental technology industry is one example, whose business is assisted by regulations requiring industry to operate cleaner processes and emission-reduction technologies. In this respect, the Environmental Industries Commission (EIC) has suggested (80) that *"substantial"* new jobs opportunities may result from the increased use of cleaner technologies, and that international studies show that generally more jobs are created than lost as a result of investing in environmental technologies. The EU has suggested that environmental improvement policy could create 3-4 million jobs throughout the EU by 2000 (although the money spent on environmental technologies could have been spent elsewhere, creating jobs in other sectors of the economy). Overall it is dangerous to generalise, but on a macro-economic scale, many believe the outcome will be less negative than assumed in the guidance, which envisages regulations resulting only in costs to business; the balance of costs and benefits could be economically neutral or even positive when the net financial gains of the environmental technology industries are taken into account.

There are also examples where **regulations can actually reduce costs to business,** rather than increasing them. Indeed, Green Business Clubs have taken off in a number of areas in England, and the Aire and Calder Project and Project Catalyst are two specific examples where industries have reduced waste and emissions in order to comply with regulations, and consequently reduced their costs considerably (59). The Government has recognised the value of these schemes, and in its strategy for sustainable waste management (60), seeks to promote their growth - citing the cost savings that can result as a positive reason for reducing waste.

Environmental and consumer groups thus see the Deregulation Initiative as creating something of an 'unlevel' playing field on which future regulatory decisions will be made. Not only may the net costs be overestimated in some cases, but the guidance's emphasis on discounted costs makes it easier to quantify (and attach greater weight to) the short-term costs of implementation and regulation, than the environmental benefits. CPRE has questioned whether, for example, it should be the role of the Environment Agency to consider the competitiveness of industry, but more generally the question is raised over how far risk assessment and management processes in the environmental field will have to change in response to the initiative, and **how far the initiatives will drive the Agency towards adopting the more narrow interpretation of cost-benefit analysis and risk assessment required under deregulation, rather than taking the broader view emerging in the constituent parts of the Agency,** and those envisaged in the DoE's own guidance (Section 3.4.5, Box 3.5).

In this respect, the current Deregulation Unit guidance recognises that in some departments, specific guidance is already available, and it *"is not intended to replace or alter"* this. However, concerns remain over differences in emphasis between the different sources of guidance in the field of environmental protection. One aspect is the cost emphasis already described, but a second is over the apparent lower priority given in the Unit's guidance to public perception considerations. This reserves matters of perception for explicit Ministerial judgement, which could be seen as creating a potential tension with the trends in HSE and the Agency for greater participation and consideration of public perception from the outset in their regulatory processes. The Deregulation Unit has indicated that its guidance will be updated and **this would present an opportunity to clarify the significance of these differences.**

4.4   Research Needs

The previous discussion considered how the Environment Agency might use risk assessment in fulfilling its objectives and identified a number of limitations in current decision-making processes. **How then, are the current methods to be improved, taking account of the need to understand and include public perceptions of risks, but also ensuring that regulation and policy are based on sound science?** The first step is to be clear what we mean by 'sound science', since while research into the physical and natural sciences continues to represent the largest share of the research into risk (e.g. engineering failure analysis, dispersion modelling, toxicology, epidemiology and ecotoxicology), there is also an increasing trend towards research into the social science aspects. Indeed the Agriculture, Natural Resources and Environment (ANRE) Panel of the Technology Foresight exercise (81) and Government plans for science and engineering and technology (82) concluded that both natural and social sciences have a role to play in improving decision-making and regulation. In this context, it would be necessary to combine these two schools of thought in multidisciplinary research programmes that can bring together the natural scientists' understanding of the world and the social scientists' approach to identifying bias, subjectivity, perceptions and values.

In the Social Sciences, the Economic and Social Research Council (ESRC) has developed a programme of research into risk and human behaviour and similarly, the HSE has sponsored research into public perceptions of risks associated with particularly hazardous sites, and the monetary valuation of safety benefits (**Box 4.2**). Many academics are actively researching into risk perception, risk communication, and alternative decision-making processes, and much of this research requires input from many disciplines, spanning both the social and natural sciences - recognising the importance of both schools in consideration of risk assessment and decision-making.

BOX 4.2 MULTI-DISCIPLINARY RESEARCH INTO RISK

ESRC Risk and Human Behaviour Research Programme

ESRC has developed a £3M, 5-year research programme comprising 25 projects, involving the full range of social science disciplines, and including collaboration with other disciplines in a number of cases. Fourteen projects have been commissioned initially, with another 10-12 due to be launched in Autumn 1996.

The aims of the programme are to shed more light on how people behave in the face of risk by supporting research which promotes:

- Advances in the theoretical and conceptual frameworks of risk.
- Multidisciplinary research between social scientists, and where appropriate, between the social and natural sciences.
- Policy and practical applications in the public and private sectors.
- Integration between fields of study such as the personal, social and cultural aspects of risk.

Of particular interest in the context of this report, projects in the programme include:

- A cognitive theory of risk-taking behaviour.
- Effects of emotion and other state changes on personal risk behaviour.
- From precautionary to risk-based regulation: the case of GMO releases.
- Media and expert constructions of risk.
- Redefining the cultural context of risk perception.

Health and Safety Executive Study

In May 1995, the HSE commissioned a 3-year, multidisciplinary study of the public perception of risks associated with major hazard sites, which aims to consider:

- how people express their perceptions of risk;
- how stable those perceptions might be;
- which factors are significant in shaping how the public sees risk;
- how policy-makers can be helped to understand and respond to public perceptions of risk.

Also, the project aims to explore a number of issues central to risk research, including:

- how diverse and consistent are the views held by different groups in society;
- how national and local factors influence perceptions of risk;
- the role of trust and public credibility of regulators and industry;
- how significant are people's sense of empowerment or powerlessness, and their participation in decision-making.

The main outcome of the project will be to provide the HSE and other government departments with a deeper understanding of how different sectors of the public understand and perceive the risks associated with major hazard sites. Also, the project aims to make its findings widely available, and will run seminars across the country to present and discuss the results.

HSE is also sponsoring a project (in conjunction with the Department of Transport, the Home Office and the Treasury) to look at the monetary valuation of safety benefits across a range of risk areas, i.e. transport safety, radiation, sport and leisure, genetically-modified organisms, occupational health and fire safety.

Within the **Environment Agency**, research will (for the short-term at least) continue along the lines pursued by the predecessors. For instance, the NRA research programme included a number of projects looking at risk analysis, economic appraisal and environmental impact assessment. Similarly HMIP's Centre for Integrated Environmental Risk Assessment (CIERA) and Environmental Assessment Centre looked at ways of developing and promoting more transparent risk assessment approaches, such as the Operator and Pollution Risk Appraisal (OPRA) scheme and the Integrated Environmental Index (IEI) technique for defining the BPEO for a process (described in Section 3).

Much of this work has been based on developing numerical 'scientific' approaches to risk assessment, rather than taking account of the psychological and cultural aspects involved in perceptions of risk, and in building and maintaining the public's trust in regulators and decision-makers. The question is thus raised of how far the new remit to promote open, inclusive, two-way communication will cause the research agenda **to encompass the emerging importance of the social science aspects of risk assessment and decision-making.**

The Agency's R&D programme has not yet been agreed, but early indications are that improving the ways in which risks are assessed will form an important part of its strategy. Recognising that its predecessors assessed risks differently, the Agency is hoping to broaden the remit of the CIERA (which it inherited from HMIP). Thus, it hopes extend the traditional engineering/science approach to incorporate life sciences and social factors such as economics, psychology and sociology (79). Also, the Centre for Hazard and Risk Manage-ment at Loughborough University is completing a study for the Agency on waste manage-ment and public communication. Early indications are that some component parts of the Agency **suffer from very low levels of public trust**, and so it may be useful for the Agency to determine for itself how the public perceives its role, mandates policies and methods.

4.5 In Conclusion

Risk assessment is being used more often in decision-making, because of an increased need to deal with uncertainties more systematically and to improve the regulatory system. More specifically, the emerging Environment Agency aims to create a new culture; bringing together the best aspects of its predecessors (HMIP, the NRA, the WRAs and some units from DoE), and Government guidance requires the Agency to base its decisions on sound science, while also taking account of uncertainties, and the need to work towards sustainable development.

These changes are set against the backdrop of questions concerned over **how far science can contribute to decision-making in the face of uncertainty** and more emphasis too on 'risk psychology' in decision-making. While no single method could arrive at universally acceptable decisions, many conclude that **decision-making should be open, accountable and inclusive; seeking to achieve consensus; and taking proper account of both the natural and social scientific dimensions of risk.**

The importance of risk assessment and its public acceptability has been illustrated on several occasions in the last year. Thus, from the Brent Spar episode (83, 84), Shell UK has acknowledged that "*technocratic compliance with rational, science-based regulation is not, in itself, enough.*" Comparative risks also feature widely in public debate ranging from the dangers of drugs such as ecstasy to the risks of eating beef.

In view of the importance of **credibility and trust in generating public confidence in the management of risks**, its is hoped that this review will be useful to Parliamentarians who must deal on a day to day basis with the public's perception of risks.

REFERENCES

1   Department of the Environment, Ministry of Agriculture, Fisheries and Food and Welsh Office, 1995. The Environment Agency and Sustainable Development. December 1995.

2   Royal Commission on Environmental Pollution, 1988. Twelfth Report: Best Practicable Environmental Option. Cm 310. London: HMSO.

3   House of Commons Environment Select Committee, 1989. Session 1983-89 Second Report. Toxic Waste, February 1989. HC Paper 22. London: HMSO.

4   Parliamentary Office of Science and Technology, 1993. Contaminated Land, October 1993.

5   House of Lords Select Committee on Sustainable Development, 1995. Session 1994-5. volume 1 - Report HL72, June 1995. London: HMSO.

6   Department of the Environment, 1990. This Common Inheritance. Britain's Environmental Strategy. cm1200. London: HMSO.

7   World Commission on Environment and Development, 1987. Our Common Future. Oxford University Press.

8   Department of the Environment, 1994. Sustainable Development: The UK Strategy. Cm 2426. London: HMSO.

9   Health and Safety Executive, 1995. Generic Terms and Concepts in the Assessment and Regulation of Industrial Risks.

10   Warner, F., 1992. Introduction. In: Risk: Analysis, Perception and Management. Report of a Royal Society Study Group. The Royal Society.

11   Soby, B.A., Simpson, A.C.D. & Ives, D.P., 1993. Integrating Public and Scientific Judgements into a Tool-kit for Managing Food-Related Risks. Stage 1: Literature Review and Feasibility Study. Centre for Environmental Risk Management, World Health Organisation Collaborating Centre on Environmental Health Risk Assessment and Communication. Research Report No. 16. School of Environmental Sciences, University of East Anglia, December 1993.

12   Department of the Environment, 1995. A Guide to Risk Assessment and Risk Management for Environmental Protection. London: HMSO.

13   Fischoff, B., Slovic, P., Lichtenstein, S., Reed, S. and Coombs, B., 1978. How Safe is Safe Enough? A Psychometric Study of Attitudes Towards Technological Risks and Benefits. Policy Sciences, Vol. 9, pp 127-152.

14   Lofstedt, R.E., Evaluation of the siting of two waste tyre incinerators: one successful and one unsuccessful example. Risk Research Centre, Centre for Environmental Strategy, University of Surrey. Forthcoming.

15   Parliamentary Office of Science and Technology, 1995. Public Attitudes to Science. POSTnote 69, November 1995.

16   Marris, C., Langford, I. and O'Riordan, T., 1996. Integrating Sociological and Psychological Approaches to Public Perceptions of Environmental Risks: Detailed Results from a Questionnaire Survey. CSERGE Working Paper GEC 96-07. Centre for Social and Economic Research on Global Environment, University of East Anglia.

17   Risk-Benefit Working Group, 1995. Risk-Benefit Analysis of Existing Substances. Chemical Industries Association, London.

18   Risk & Policy Analysts Limited and Acer Environmental, 1993.   Risk-Benefit Analysis of Hazardous Chemicals.   Final Report to the Department of the Environment, December 1992. London: HMSO.

19   Wynne, B., 1989.   Frameworks of Rationality in Risk Management: Towards the Testing of Naive Sociology.   In: Environmental Threats: Perception, Analysis and Management.   Brown, J. (ed).   Economic and Social Research Council, Belhaven Press.

20   Advisory Committee on Business and the Environment, 1996. Sixth Progress Report to and Response from the President of the Board of Trade and the Secretary of State for the Environment. April 1996. Department of Trade and Industry.

21   Parliamentary Office of Science and Technology, 1996.   BSE and CJD: Science, Uncertainty and Risk. POST Technical Report 78, April 1996.

22   National Radiological Protection Board, 1989.   Living With Radiation.   London: HMSO.

23   Baines, J., 1995.   Beyond Compromise: Building Consensus in Environmental Planning and Decision-making. The Environment Council, London.

24   Robinson, S., 1995. "Actually It's Not As Simple As That..." Paper presented at the Environment Council seminar Understanding the Changing Environmental Agenda: A Company Survival Guide, Royal Horticultural Halls, London, 29 September 1995.

25   Robinson, S., 1996.   Out of the Twilight Zone.   Managing the Threats and Opportunities of an Environmentally Sustainable Business.   The Environment Council, London.

26   Lofstedt, R.E., 1995. Risk Evaluation in the United Kingdom: Legal Requirements, Conceptual Foundations, and Practical Experiences with Special Emphasis on Energy Systems. Centre for Environmental Strategy, University of Surrey, April 1995.

27   Parliamentary Office of Science and Technology, 1995. Transport: Some Issues in Sustainability, November 1995.

28   Department of Transport, 1996. Transport - The Way Forward. The Government's Response to the Transport Debate. Cm 3234, April 1996. London: HMSO.

29   O'Riordan, T., 1995. The Precautionary Principle. Environmental Values, Vol 4, No. 3., 1995.

30   Johnston, P., Santillo, D. and Stringer, R., 1996.   Risk Assessment and Reality: Recognizing the Limitations. In: Environmental Impact of Chemicals: Assessment and Control.   Quint, M., Purchase, R. and Taylor, D. (eds).   Royal Society of Chemistry, 1996.

31   Pidgeon, N., et al., 1992. Risk Perception. In: Risk: Analysis, Perception and Management. Report of a Royal Society Study Group. London, The Royal Society, 1992.

34   Hood, C.C., et al., 1992. Risk Management. In: Risk: Analysis, Perception and Management. Report of a Royal Society Study Group. London, The Royal Society, 1992.

33   Adams, J., 1995. Risk. London: UCL Press.

34   Beck, U., 1992. Risk Society. London: Sage.

35   Brown, J., 1989.   Introduction: Approaches, Tools and Perceptions.   In: Environmental Threats: Perception, Analysis and Management. Brown, J. (ed). Economic and Social Research Council, Belhaven Press.

36   The Environment Council, 1994. The Essential Environmental Mediator and Facilitator. Course Handbook.

37   Simmons, P. and Marris, C., 1995. Combining Qualitative and Quantitative Research Methods. Report of an ESRC-sponsored Workshop on Qualitative Research Methods in the Study of Public Risk Perceptions. Newsletter of the Risk Communication Network, Vol. 1, No. 3, October 1995. Centre for Environmental and Risk Management, University of East Anglia.

38   Phillip, R., 1996. Qualitative and Quantitative Research. Newsletter of the Risk Communication Network, Vol. 1, No. 4, January 1996. Centre for Environmental and Risk Management, University of East Anglia.

39   Petts, J., 1995. Waste Management Strategy Development: A Case Study of Community Involvement and Consensus - Building in Hampshire. Journal of Environmental Planning and Management, vol. 38, No. 4, 1995

40   Interdepartmental Liaison Group on Risk Assessment, 1996. Use of Risk Assessment within Government Departments. Health and Safety Executive, January 1996.

41   ETSU, 1996. Integration of Consensus-building into the Planning Process for Renewable Energy Schemes. Project Profile 403, February 1996, Department of Trade and Industry.

42   Department of Trade and Industry, 1993   Regulation in the Balance   A Guide to Risk Assessment. The Deregulation Initiative, November 1993.

43   Cabinet Office, 1996. Checking the Cost of Regulation. A Guide to Compliance Cost Assessment. HMSO, London.

44   Cabinet Office, 1996. Regulation in the Balance. A Guide to Regulatory Appraisal Incorporating Risk Assessment. HMSO: London.

45   Pearce, D. and Turner, K., 1992. Benefits Estimates and Environmental Decision-Making. Report for the Organisation for Economic Co-operation and Development (OECD). Centre for Social and Economic Research on the Global Environment (CSERGE), London, 1992.

46   Adams, J., 1995. Cost-Benefit Analysis: Part of the problem, not the solution. Report for the Green College Centre for Environmental Policy and Understanding, Green College, Oxford.

47   Department of the Environment, Scottish Office and Welsh Office, 1995. Review of Radioactive Waste Management Policy, Cm 2919. London: HMSO.

48   Health and Safety Executive, 1992. The Tolerability of Risk from Nuclear Power Stations. London: HMSO.

49   The Royal Society, 1994   Disposal of Radioactive Wastes in Deep Repositories. Report of a Royal Society Study Group, November 1994.

50   Royal Commission on Environmental Pollution, 1976. 5th Report. Air Pollution Control: An Integrated Approach. Cm 6371, January 1976.

51   Department of the Environment and Welsh Office, 1991. Integrated Pollution Control: A Practical Guide. May 1991.

52   Her Majesty's Inspectorate of Pollution, undated. Environmental, Economic and BPEO Assessment principles for Integrated Pollution Control. Technical Guidance Note E1 (Environment).

53   Anon, 1995. Questions Persist over HMIP's BPEO Assessment Method. ENDS Report 251, December 1995, pp. 27-28.

54   National Rivers Authority, 1995. Water Quality Strategy.

55   Her Majesty's Inspectorate of Pollution, 1995. Operator and Pollution Risk Appraisal (OPRA), April 1995.

56   National Rivers Authority, 1995. Flood Defence Strategy.

57   Department of the Environment, 1994. Licensing of Waste Management Facilities. Waste Management Paper No. 4. London: HMSO.

58   Department of the Environment, 1995. Landfill Design, Construction and Operational Practice. Waste Management Paper No. 26B. London: HMSO.

59   Parliamentary Office of Science and Technology, 1994. Waste Disposal and Recycling - Overview and Issues. An Analysis for the House of Lords Committee on Sustainable Development, December 1994.

60   Department of the Environment and the Welsh Office, 1995. Making Waste Work. A Strategy for Sustainable Waste Management in England And Wales. Cm 3040. London: HMSO.

61   House of Commons Environment Committee, 1990. Contaminated Land. First Report Session 1989-90. HC 170. London: HMSO.

62   Parliamentary Office of Science and Technology, 1995. Bathing Water Directive. Review of Proposal Modifications for House of Commons European Legislation Committee.

63   Health and Safety Executive, 1995. A Social Regulator's Use of Science. Paper given by JD Rimmington, Director General, HSE at The Royal Society Discussion Meeting on Extrapolation of Dose Response Data, 7 July 1995.

64   International Environmental Technology Centre, 1996. Environmental Risk Assessment for Sustainable Cities. Technical Publication Series, No. 3. United Nations Environment Programme. Osaka/Shiga, 1996.

65   Warner, F., 1995. Process Safety and Environmental Protection. Trans IChemE, Vol 73, Part B, November 1995, Supplement.

66   National Research Council, 1983. Risk Assessment in the Federal Government: Managing the Process. Washington, D.C. National Academy Press.

67   Ball, D.J. and Stern, R.M., 1992. Risk Communication: Dealing with the Spectrum of Environment and Health Risks in Europe. Report of a World Health Organisation Consultation, Ulm, 28-30 November 1990. Centre for Environmental Risk Management, World Health Organisation Collaborating Centre on Environmental Health Risk Assessment and Communication. Research Report No. 11. School of Environmental Sciences, University of East Anglia, April 1992.

68   Anon., 1996. Assessing Environmental Risks: Why Science Alone is Not Enough. Public Policy Issues. Greenpeace Business, February/March 1996, p.7.

69   Lofstedt, R.E., 1995. Why are Public Perception Studies on the Environment Ignored? Global Environmental Change, Vol. 5, No. 2, pp.83-85, 1995.

70   Parliamentary Office of Science and Technology, 1996. BSE and CJD: Science, Uncertainty and Risk. Technical Report 78, April 1996.

71   Parliamentary Office of Science and Technology, 1995. Plant Biotechnology - A Consensus? POSTnote 56, January 1995.

72   UK Round Table on Sustainable Development, 1996. First Annual Report, April 1996.

73   Local Government Management Board, Local Agenda 21 Principles and Process, A Step by Step Guide.

74   Slater, D., 1996. Speech made at the first public briefing by the Environment Agency at the Queen Elizabeth II Conference Centre, London, 6 February 1996.

75   Council for the Protection of Rural England, 1996. Environment Agency - Draft Guidance. Response by the Council for the Protection of Rural England. January 1996.

76   Department of the Environment, 1991. Policy Appraisal and the Environment. A Guide for Government Departments. London: HMSO.

77   Her Majesty's Inspectorate of Pollution, 1995. The Application of Risk Assessment and Risk Management to Integrated Pollution Control. Review of Current Practice. Centre for Intgrated Environmental Risk Assessment (CIERA) Report Number 1.

78   Her Majesty's Inspectorate of Pollution, 1995. Centre for Integrated Environmental Risk Assessment. Department of the Environment.

79   Environment Agency, 1996. Centre for Integrated Environmental Risk Assessment - Draft Business Plan.

80   Wilkes, A., 1995. The World of Opportunities for the Environmental Industry. Environmental Industries Commission, April 1995.

81   Office of Science and Technology, 1995. Technology Foresight. Report No. 11, Agriculture, Natural Resources and Environment. Cabinet Office. London: HMSO.

82   Office of Science and Technology, 1995. Forward Look of Government-funded Science, Engineering and Technology, 1995 Cabinet Office. London: HMSO.

83   Parliamentary Office of Science and Technology, 1995. Oil 'Rig' Disposal. POSTnote 65, July 1995.

84   Faulds, E., 1996. Why is Brent Spar Unique? A Speech to the Institute of Petroleum Conference on Minimising the Impact of Decommissioning, London, 22 February 1996. Shell UK Exploration and Production.

GLOSSARY

ACBE	Advisory Committee on Business and the Environment
ACSNI	Advisory Committee on the Safety of Nuclear Installations
ACTS	Advisory Committee on Toxic Substances
ALARP	As Low As Reasonably Practicable
ANRE	Agriculture, Natural Resources and Environment
ARCI	Alkali and Radiochemical Inspectorate (Northern Ireland)
BATNEEC	Best Available Techniques Not Entailing Excessive Cost
BEO	Best Environmental Option
BPEO	Best Practicable Environmental Option
BPM	Best Practicable Means
BSE	Bovine Spongiform Encephalopathy
CBA	Cost-Benefit Analysis
CBI	Confederation of British Industry
CCA	Compliance-Cost Assessment
CERM	Centre for Environmental and Risk Management
CFC	Chlorofluorocarbon
CIERA	Centre for Integrated Environmental Risk Management
CJD	Creutzfeld Jakob Disease
COMARE	Committee on the Medical Aspects of Radiation in the Environment
CPRE	Council for the Protection of Rural England
DoE	Department of the Environment
DoT	Department of Transport
DTF	Deregulation Task Force
DTI	Department of Trade and Industry
DWI	Drinking Water Inspectorate
EAL	Environmental Action Level
EC	European Commission
EIC	Environmental Industries Commission
EQ	Environmental Quotient
EQS	Environmental Quality Standard
ESRC	Economic and Social Research Council
ETSU	Energy Technology Support Unit
GMO	Genetically-Modified Organism
HCFC	Hydrochlorofluorocarbon
HFC	Hydrofluorocarbon
HMIP	Her Majesty's Inspectorate of Pollution (England and Wales)
HMIPI	Her Majesty's Industrial Pollution Inspectorate (Scotland)
HSC	Health and Safety Commission
ICRCL	Interdepartmental Committee on the Redevelopment of Contaminated Land
IEI	Integrated Environmental Index
ILGRA	Inter-departmental Liaison Group on Risk Assessment
IPC	Integrated Pollution Control
IRAC	Ionising Radiations Advisory Committee
IRBM	Integrated River Basin Management
NRA	National Rivers Authority

NRPB	National Radiological Protection Board
NSCA	National Society for Clean Air and Environmental Protection
OEL	Occupational Exposure Limit
OFWAT	Office of Water Services
OPRA	Operator Pollution Risk Assessment
PEC	Predicted Environmental Concentration
PP	Precautionary Principle
QRA	Quantitative Risk Assessment
RCEP	Royal Commission on Environmental Pollution
RWMAC	Radioactive Waste Management Advisory Committee
SEPA	Scottish Environmental Protection Agency
SEPAC	Statutory Environmental Protection Advisory Committee
ToR	Tolerability of Risk
WRA	Waste Regulation Authority